THE TEENAGE WORRIER'S GUIDE TO LURVE

www.booksattransworld.co.uk/childrens

Other zany titles available from Ros Asquith
and published by Corgi Books

I WAS A TEENAGE WORRIER
THE TEENAGE WORRIER'S GUIDE TO LIFE
THE TEENAGE WORRIER'S WORRY FILES
THE PANICK DIARY

THE TEENAGE WORRIER'S Guide to LURVE

Ros Asquith.

as Letty Chubb, aged fifteen

CORGI BOOKS

To Teenage Worriers everywhere

THE TEENAGE WORRIER'S GUIDE TO LURVE
A CORGI BOOK : 0 552 14339 1

First publication in Great Britain

PRINTING HISTORY
Corgi edition published 1996

7 9 10 8

Copyright © 1996 by Ros Asquith

The right of Ros Asquith to be identified as the author of
this work has been asserted in accordance with the
Copyright, Designs and Patents Act 1988

Condition of Sale
This book is sold subject to the condition that it shall not,
by way of trade or otherwise, be lent, re-sold, hired out or
otherwise circulated without the publisher's prior consent in any
form of binding or cover other than that in which it is published
and without a similar condition including this condition being
imposed on the subsequent purchaser.

Set in 11½pt Linotype Garamond 3 by Phoenix Typesetting,
Ilkley, West Yorkshire.

Corgi Books are published by Transworld Publishers,
61–63 Uxbridge Road, Ealing, London W5 5SA,
a division of The Random House Group Ltd,
in Australia by Random House Australia (Pty) Ltd,
20 Alfred Street, Milsons Point, Sydney, NSW 2061, Australia,
in New Zealand by Random House New Zealand Ltd,
18 Poland Road, Glenfield, Auckland 10, New Zealand
and in South Africa by Random House (Pty) Ltd,
Endulini, 5a Jubilee Road, Parktown 2193, South Africa.

Printed and bound in Great Britain by
Cox & Wyman Ltd, Reading, Berkshire.

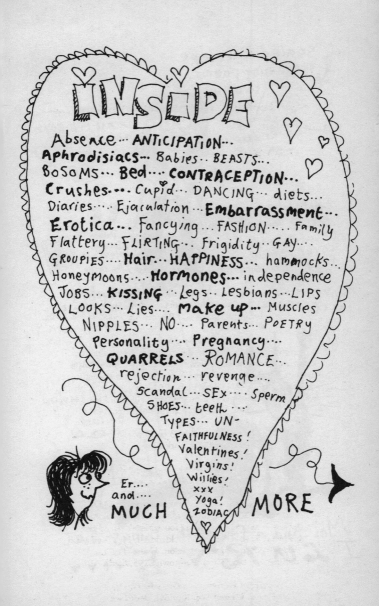

A Pile of Old Socks
Festering room
Crumbly Apology for a Home
What is fancifully known as a street
Capital(ist) City
Titchy Britain (all alone in a vast ocean, sob)
Glorious but tragically threatened planet
Solar System
Outer Space
Other Galaxies
Infinity
The great Unknown.

Dearest Reader(s),

This handy volume is about Loof, luv, lerve, lurve and even Love in all its many varieties, and any seedy Teenage Worriers looking for a book about sexual intercourse, willies, heaving bods, fluorescent condoms Etck Etck should look along the top shelves of their newsagent or on page 256, and maybe run a cold shower as well, just like I think I'd better do before I go any further.

Er, it's embarrassing I know, but have you ever been in Love?

You know, when the Object of Your Desire says 'hi' and you write it in your diary? Wonder what it would sound like set to music? Conclude that it couldn't be more beeyoootiful music than it is already, more romantic than Elgar, more erotic than Take That (OK, maybe that isn't so hard), more torrential than Pavarotti in the bath Etck?

1

Do you gaze dreamily at sunsets, moonscapes Etck wondering why you never noticed the Glory of our Natural Universe before?

Do you discover that your Lurve Object's favourite colour is mustard and rush out for the dye even though you wreck five saucepans and all your T-shirts in the process and end up looking like a frankfurter?

Do you start writing poetry and thinking it's GOOD?

These are signs of the REAL THING.

But I will warn you straightaway, there is V. Little you can do to capture your Loved One's Love.

This book is about that V. Little. And it is much better for the soul to do V. Little than nothing. I think.

I'm doing it as an alphabet 'cos it's easier, er, I mean more accessible, *and because (blush, massive dollop of modesty Etck Etck) although none of my uncaring family (with the honourable exception of daaaaaaarling Granny Chubb) have looked at my previous tome I WAS A TEENAGE WORRIER, you, my dear fellow worriers, have sent in male (whoops, must hurl mangy frame into cold shower ASAP),* sorry, mail *by the sackful imploring me to do another. Gosh.*

But can I live down to your expectations?

I cannot in all honesty say that I have relinquished Doom, Gloom and Guilt (sounds like a firm of lawyers, or maybe undertakers) or that I have banished Worry from my life. I have not, sadly, become the skittish, devil-may-care, take-it-or-leave-it, lurve-'em-and-leave-'em person I dream of being.

And the reason for this, my dear fellows in struggle, is LURVE (I'm certain I could sort out my parents, school, spots, animal welfare, friends, socks, ecology Etck Etck if I

*could only conquer this one crucial five billion megaton
Superworry, which is throwing out deadly nausea-inducing
background radiation twenty-four hours a day, and
occasionally goes into Melt Down without warning at Bad
Times, like Exams, or when you're trying to give a manicure
to the cat).*

*Naturally, when I have put into practice all the handy
tips in this invaluable tome you are now holding, I will be
IRRESISTIBLE. I will be just like my noble, brilliant,
V.V. Handsome brother Ashley (moan, envy, gnash) and I
will finally be able to swap yearning for spurning. Heh heh
heh, mad cackle of triumph Etck.*

*And it will work for you, too! You've read this far in the
bookshop, so dig into your pocket and SPEND, SPEND,
SPEND! Live a little! Buy a book!*

*What do you mean you've only got a bit of gum with a
filling in it, a dead bus ticket and a tissue on which is
written the innermost thoughts of your hooter? CAMPAIGN
FOR FREE BOOKS! (also condoms, clothes, nosh Etck Etck.)*

*One other thing. Carnal LURVE, world shattering
though it may be, is not the only kind of lurve. So I have
included other bits of lurve in here, like FRENDZ (if you're
lucky enough to have some that don't steal your Loved One off
you), FAMILY (I know I've got two parents and two
brothers and some of you haven't got anyone at all (sob,
violins, howl of wolves Etck) but maybe you've got a friendly
social worker), PETS (I am getting more allergic by the day,
but sometimes I think my cat Rover is the only person who'll
ever Truly Care — must give her a hug — a-a-a-a-achoo) as
all these things can be a comfort to the agonized recipient of*

unrequited passion. And Soothe the Savage Beast, sorry, breast).

So, dear, anguished reader(s) . . . I hope you can enjoy this Alphabet of LURVE and find a little glimpse of sunshine in the clouds, of laughter amid the tears Etck. I would love to be able to deal with everything, but I have to go by my own vast experience which so far does not include actual DOING IT, or for that matter how to cope with a LURVED ONE who wants to Do It upside down wearing only a wetsuit, a string of onions, a bald wig and a carrot up his nose with Kim Basinger's photo stuck to it with blu-tak. I think I might leave that kind of advice to politicians, tabloid newspapers Etck.

Still, if there is something urgent I should have included, please don't hesitate to write in so I may add it to the, ahem, revised edition.

LURVERS OF THE WORLD UNTIE!
I mean, Unite.

Love (ah, that word again)

ER, JUST A LITTLE UPDATE ON MY FAMILY,
FRENDZ ETCK.

UPDATE . . . MOI
SCARLETT JANE CHUBB

Still 15 yrs old (feel 95, specially when watching
Granny Chubb do housework). Still V. Lanky. I am
sure I have grown three cm in the last month but I
can't find a ruler long enough and my adored father's
fold-up-and-rip-your-finger-off steel tape is jammed
with emulsion, which must be a relief to the local
privatized hospital's overstretched casualty Dept,
currently running on a piece of gum with a filling in it,
a dead bus ticket Etck Etck.

My nose is also growing; must check with Doc to see
if this is Normal. My nickname will probably soon
change from Concorde to whatever that new Super-
Plane's called that will get to Australia in 45 mins by
going via Jupiter. If *Neighbours* is anything to go by,
who wants to go there anyway . . .

Luckily, the other thing that grows fast is my wig,
which I can nearly hide behind again after cropping to
impress my Loved One (cringe, fat-lot-of-good Etck).
But do I *want* to hide behind a mat of wholewheat
spaghetti? It is questions like this that this humble
tome is designed to answer.

I have abandoned photography classes full of
talentless, soulless people like Aggy, and continue my
relationship with my camera alone (but I am having

second thoughts as it is a KIDDIES' FIRST SNAPS job I got when I was 8 and does not seem to have the magical properties of the Nikax Superzoom, Virtual Reality, Artificial Intelligence, Overnight Fame single lens reflex they let us borrow at the classes).

I have temporarily postponed my ambition to be a Nun and give up the Sins of the Flesh Etck. This is because 1) I never got a reply to my letter asking how to be a Nun — maybe they take a Vow Of Rudeness and 2) I thought, how can you give up something until you've tried it?

I will be a film director first. When I am world famous I will give it all up at a modest press conference by donating my penthouses to the poor (except, say, three of them) and become a Buddhist Nun.

OK, I've put off admitting this. But there is one I Lurve.

It is still He.

Daniel.

I know that when I finished my last book I thought his hair looked like rubber bands, but I now know the colour of wet sand and the colour of rubber bands are worlds apart.

He is the most noble, kind, true and good person in the Universe (also V.V. Handsome, which I can take or leave, of course). Sorry, got a bit over-the-top there. Put away the sick bag, dab yourself with Kleenex and read on . . . we'll get back to **Daniel Hope** later . . . (can you bear to wait????)

UPDATE . . . MOTHER
Alice Constance Gosling

('If it hadn't been for having children I could have been a great ARTIST' Etck Yawn)

Those of you who read the best-selling I WAS A TEENAGE WORRIER (advert, plug, puff Etck) may have gathered from the fact that I still need loadsadosh that my Mother's contract to design wallpaper has not kept the Wolf from the Door. In fact the Wolf has even got IN, as all the home furnishings manufacturers who came round wanted was to make Evil Suggestions to my only mother, and her a Parent and Ancient Person and everything.

She hates her job at the kiddies' library, having been Born-to-Better-Things and still cannot understand why the bank won't just give her money when she wants it, like her father used to do. It is V. Worrying the way she spends a fortune she hasn't got on some daft thing like a trellis (our 'garden' is a four-foot patio) and then panics and cancels the milk.

She is also convinced that my ickle brother Benjy is dyslexic. I tell her no-one reads novels at 5 except children who were forced to watch Open University videos in their baby-bouncers, given the Oxford edition of Thomas The Tank Engine with extensive footnotes, and who can repeat the chemical formula for powdered milk. This brings on a bout of breast-beating Worry about her ickle darlings' education and how I will never get my GCSEs if I stay on at dreaded Sluggs Comprehensive.

My mum thinks the answer to life's Great Questions is a new oven, but I know DIFFERENT. And when I make zillions of quid from my writing (ahem) I will buy her one and then she will understand that Life's Pain is not stilled by being able to over-boil the sprouts even faster.

UPDATE . . . FATHER
Leonard Anthony Chubb

('If it hadn't been for having KIDS I'd have been a great WRITER" Etck. Sigh.)

My father's Great Unwritten Novel is proceeding apace. It moved all the way from the drawer of his desk to the bin when he fell off a ladder changing a light-bulb, but he rescued most of it, which wasn't difficult because it's about four pages as far as I can see.

But where there's Life there's Hope. It's just that the silence that comes from my father's 'study' makes me worry whether life exists within. Occasionally a strange high-pitched keening sound comes out, and when I tiptoe to the door and peep through the keyhole I see he is hunched over his computer.

Is this the final burst, the Explosion of Energy that will carry him, modestly waving to the glowing hordes, all the way to the Noble Prize for Litt, Booker Prize for Books Etck? No, he is playing *DOLPHS,* a New-Age computer game where you have to rescue good brainy mammals (dolphins) from bad brainy mammals (us), and when you get to the last level the dolphins buy the humans veggiburgers and Evian all round, let bygones be bygones, and everybody has a good old ultrasonic laugh about it. It is all V. Nice compared to Zappem and Mincem games and it has won wildlife preservation awards Etck. But how will we eat?

UPDATE . . . BROTHER 1
Ashley (18)

Still V. Handsome, brainy, kind, faultless Etck Etck gnash grr. At University so although it's a relief not to have to compare myself with him daily, I miss him (aaaah). NB Several Teenage Worriers have enquired whether Ashley is available. Sadly, he is engaged to be married. But given the high divorce rate in our crumbling nation I will keep you posted.

UPDATE . . . BROTHER 2
Benjy (5)

Aaaah, bless. Butter wouldn't melt Etck Etck. But I have an armful of scratches, bites, bruises, weals, scabs, sores, cuts, injuries, traumas, lacerations, lesions, gashes, abrasions, contusions, scars (who needs a Thesaurus when you've got *moi*?) to prove different. I tried contacting the NSPCC and they sent round a child abuse officer to interview my dad. They were about to haul Benjy off into care, but I managed to convince them I was the victim and Benjy the perpetrator. My Mother says it's just a phase, to do with starting Big School Etck Etck. I suppose her

11

inability to provide us with good nosh and clean clothes and my dad's insolvency are just phases, too. It's a comforting thought.

But when Benjy-Wenjy has a bad dream and comes to Letty-Poo 'cos his parents are snoring too loud to hear him and has a lickle cuddle and needs his daaaaarling Big Sister, then, aaaaaah BLESS.

UPDATE . . . PETS
Horace, Rover and Kitty

Horace remains the least attractive gerbil known to humanity, or to other gerbils for that matter, which is why he's so keen to hang on to us as the best chance he's got. I wish Benjy would get a nice boa constrictor, or a cockroach instead. My old cat **Rover** is still my best pal even if she does make me itch, and any few quid I scrape together goes on vets' potions for her constant ailments. CAMPAIGN for an NHS for pets. The startling originality of the name **Kitty** (our new addition) may convince you that we now have a terrapin in the family. But no, it is indeed Benjy's name for the kitten my rotten friend Aggy gave him to Atone for Her Sins (ie: pinching my true Lurve). The kitten is V. Cute, fluffy and spherical (not unlike Benjy) and gets all the top-of-the-milk, lurve Etck that shld be going to Rover. As a result, I am as unkind to it as my soft heart (and the RSPCA) will allow.

I still dream of having a horse, but with one blade of grass in our backyard and £7.45p in my Post Office Account, the gods (and the odds) seem stacked against My Dream.

UPDATE . . . GRANDMAS

I ♥ Granny Chubb True!

Apart from Rover (and Benjy when he needs me) **Granny Chubb** is the only person who really CARES. Sadly, she sometimes thinks I am a mugger as her glasses need replacing and she can't afford to go to the optician. CAMPAIGN FOR FREE EYE TESTS FOR PENSIONERS WHICH THE GOVT STOPPED A FEW YEARS AGO. When I say it's me, she says that's what the wolf said to Red Riding Hood. Her place is still spotless though as she can't abandon the habits of a lifetime and if you polish all day long things are bound to shine. **Grandma Gosling** is still a snotty old bat.

UPDATE . . . FRENDZ

I have a new friend! She started at Sluggs just four weeks ago and I feel I have known her all my life. **Sarah Spiggott** is V.V. funny. Everyone wants to be her friend and she has chosen *moi*. I can't believe my luck. She loves horses, films, boyz, fudge Etck Etck, but best of all, she has a Hot Water Bottle. And we both ADMITTED IT TO EACH OTHER AFTER WE HAD ONLY KNOWN EACH OTHER FOR ONE

Best Frendz

Hazel   Aggy   Spiggy

Beauty↗ Brains↗ Wit↗

(But what do they see in Moi?)

DAY. She is just like me, only without any of the
Worries. I guess it's because she's Australian. All that
sun and no Class System (tell that to the Aborigines,
but you know what I mean). She feels the same way I
do about *Neighbours*, too. She is wildly in LURVE with
a boy from Malta but went a bit red when I said
Maltesers melt in yr mouth but not Etck. She writes to
him every day, swoon.

Hazel, of course, is still my BF, but I don't see her
every day since she went to the nobs' Academy for
Young Ladies. Her parents sent her there to keep her
away from Boyz, the evil sex-machines-from-hell, but
she is currently secretly in love with a girl, heh heh

serves them right. She remains the Most Beautiful Girl in the world, making Supermodels look like gerbils (wince, envy).

Aggy, soon-to-be-Brain-of-Britain, used to be my closest frend at Sluggs Comprehensive. Her Wicked White mother ran off with the postman leaving her Caring Black dad in charge of her and a zillion unruly siblings, so she cried on my shoulder while reading the latest cyberspace-meaning-of-Universe tomes. She was V. Shy and had never kissed anyone until she swanned off with MY True Lurve. She was V.V. nice to me after she stole Daniel off me, but has now gone V. cold. Sarah says I should steal him back. I agree. But how?

Watch this space for Big Plan.

UPDATE . . . BOYFRIENDS
(Hope springs eternal, sob)

Brian Bolt

Undeterred by cutting my nose with his specs on our one attempt at snogging, Brian ('Brain') Bolt continues to ply *moi* with poems, ballads Etck. But although his complexion is improving, I have had to say a V. firm 'no' to BB. This involved an incident with a bag of flour and a bicycle tyre that I would rather not go into.

Daniel Hope
Did I say his eyes were the colour of blue Smarties? I should have said sapphires. The pain of seeing him

entwined with Aggy has been excruciating, especially as he barely acknowledges my existence. However, Aggy is due to go and visit her mother in the West Indies, jealousy, gnash, at half-term. It is the first time she has seen her for a year. But my sympathy for Aggy has diminished since her treachery, and Spiggy and I have a plan to win Daniel back to where his true hopes and happiness lie ie, that is, with *moi*. NB For details of our **plot** see next chapter (heh heh heh).

letty Hope   Mrs. Hope   Letitia Hope.

UPDATE . . . ECCENTRICITIES *(pah)*.

Meanwhile I shall yearn, and try to drown my sorrows in my Alphabet. Remember, if the word 'banana' crops up, it means the word about dying that rhymes with 'breath' that I am too Worried to say or write. An example would be 'The noise scared her half to banana' or 'the Banana of her beloved broke her heart' Etck. Sadly, this is beginning to give me a rather fraught relationship with fruit salad.

Also, I am developing a nervous tic. Although cropping my wig did wonders for my pendiculosis (use this word if you prefer not to mention NITS) it meant I couldn't twist my fringe between my fingers. This caused stress. When I look in the mirror, the nervous tic disappears . . . if I could only film it, the doc would believe me instead of looking suicidal when she glimpses me in the waiting room. It must be 'cos I told her I had a brain tumour when it turned out the kooool beret I bought was just four sizes too small.

And now, dear Reader(s), on with the book that will buy me a horse, health, happiness, glasses for Granny Chubb, a lifetime's supply of Feline Fantasy for Rover Etck Etck.

CHAPTER ONE
AAAAAAAze

Everything is a disaster. Nobody Cares. If it wasn't for my Big Plan to recapture my True Lurve, I would pack my belongings in a small handkerchief and a few dozen carrier bags and tramp the world giving arms to the poor. (My hist. book spells this as 'alms' for some reason. How the Starving Proles are expected to have any respect for the Ruling Class when it goes round handing out things it can't even spell is a mystery to me.)

I didn't sleep a wink last night on account of Benjy dreaming he was forced to walk the gangplank into shark-infested waters. He thinks the floorboards my Father has nearly finished putting down in the kitchen are like the deck of a pirate ship. What is it with him and floors?

*The only bags I remembered to take to school were the ones under my eyes, ha ha, geddit Etck. This meant I had no money, no lunch and walked all the way home (ten whole minutes) in a downpour of hailstones the size of pool balls. Then my only father lectured me about being untogether and moaning about a spot of drizzle and how he had to walk five miles to school at the age of 6 and then make supper for his five younger siblings (yawn, guilt, in that order). By this time I was starving so I rescued my packed lunch (how did it get under my **bed**?) only to find Rover had been there already.*

*On the bright side, there's just two weeks till half-term, when Spiggy and me are going to unleash **DHAM** – that stands for **Daniel Hope Aphrodisiac Mission**. I tried to ring her to discuss some of the finer details, only to find the phone is cut off as my adored father has refused to pay the bill as a protest against Social Injustice, like why he has to live with all of us.*

I don't see why he's cross with ME about it, I never spend more than an hour or so a night on it. Maybe Benjy's phoning floor manufacturers in the States, asking if they've got any Virtual Reality floor designs that look and feel and taste like strawberry angel delight.

*My mother has booked herself into a landscape painting class. I reckon the landscape looks fine as it is, ha ha, groan, yeech Etck. Anyway, it'll be an improvement on all those sploshes and daubs, but how will we afford it? Achieved potential major cash injection into Chubb Economy by finding two quid under the bed (among remains of 'Healtho' white sliced bread, peanut butter, bent can of Phizzo, vit pills, 68 odd socks, dried felt-tips Etck Etck) but blew it on chips. Washed away by Gigantic Tidal Wave of Guilt, and resolved to start **GCSE (Granny Chubb Specs Endeavour)** by saving up, so she can start seeing the wonderful world around her and stop opening a tin of cat food every time Benjy crawls into the kitchen playing Dinosaurs. Successfully persuade Benjy to donate his massive Tyrannosaurus money-box to act as the bank for this Noble Cause, though you have to be careful putting money in as it tries to gnaw your hand off with much whirring of motors and taped howls Etck whenever you hold out coins to it.*

*Anyway, what with Operation DHAM, and Operation
GCSE I'll soon have enough Operation Experience to pass
myself off as a surgeon like that bloke who put on a white coat
and a posh voice and was allowed to perform a heart bypass,
at a major London teaching Hosp, no questions asked.
Amazing what you can do with the right accent.*

*House freezing as heating on blink. Retire early with Hot
water bottle and Rover.*

*Didn't sleep a wink 'cos of Rover's wheezing but at least it
meant I got this far with writing the Great Work that will
take us out of the poverty trap and into the glittering world of
champagne socialism which is our rightful inheritance. And
now I begin with the AAAAAAAAze.*

AARDVARK

I start with this gentle creature, dear reader, firstly to
put off all you salacious, seedy types who just bought
this book for NOOKY, snogging Etck, heh heh. Not
that Aardvarks don't have their own versions of these
practices of course, or they would become an
Endangered Species and David Attenborough would be
sploshing about in Aardvark poo Etck, going on about
how the World Wildlife Fund must invest more money
in sending them naked pictures of eager young
aardvarks to get them in The Mood Etck.

However, I have also started here for the following
V. Good reasons:

1) Being a nocturnal, termite-eating mammal it reminds me of my brother Benjy (aaaahh *bless*)

2) It's the first noun in every dictionary, and I've got to start somewhere . . .

3) It is good for a pun to your LURVED one, eg (tune of old song, ask your gran if you've never heard it) 'Aardvark a million miles for one of your smiles', arf arf.

ABSENCE

'Absence', said Somebody or Other, 'is like wind to a flame. It fans a large and extinguishes a small.' This proves that my LURVE for Daniel is a raging furnace and you, dear reader, will know that any separation makes the True Heart fonder, the False Heart wander Etck Etck.

My own theory is, if you are not sure you're in LURVE, then you aren't. But if that doesn't work for you, just try a week apart. If you find yourself eyeing up the milkman on Day One, you shld End It Now.

I should add that if you ARE sure you're in LURVE, you cld still be wrong Viz my undying Passion for Brad Pittbull, which rendered my 13th birthday (when he didn't come even after I'd posted him 365 invitations) dust, ashes Etck. V. Cringe-making episode, but proof that you don't have to have Hot Sex to Feel In LURVE. You don't even have to meet.

ADAM

N.B. Chubb's theory is that Adam ate the apple anyway. Which is why it's been stuck in his throat EVER SINCE.

According to ye Holy Bible, Adam was the first bloke to take advantage when he knocked on Eve's tree, whipped off his Calvin Klein figleaf and asked if he could just pop in for a minute. Adam and Eve are the reason we all wear clothes and get embarrassed Etck. Personally I'd be perfectly happy entwining around Daniel in Eden and wouldn't give a monkey's about some old apple . . . but maybe Adam wasn't much of a looker, so Eve thought she might at least get lunch out of it.

Adam: first bloke to take advantage

ADJECTIVES

Adjectives are V. Useful for the Teenage-Worrier-In-LURVE to describe the highs and lows of ye rollercoaster of Emotions on which you are riding, and without them, how cld Daniel have written about my 'tumultuous wig' Etck, swoon, sigh, cold shower.

e.g.s of the transforming power of the
humble Adjective

Pop eyes:
"Loominous orbs that light up galaxy"

Wig like Bird's Nest:
"Tousled, Gloriously untamed mane"

I am V. proud of my description of DH's hair as like 'wet sand at sunset' and I'm sure you'll agree it's more endearing than just plain 'sandy'. Or 'rubber bandy' which is doubtless what a person not in LURVE with DH wld think of his wig. LURVE is a great transformer. Viz. V. small person with V. Big hooter becomes, in the eyes of their LURVEr, 'petite, with a commanding profile'. Aaaah.

AIDS: see STDs

AISLE

This is where many Teenage Worriers-in-LURVE think they will walk up to make promises they can't keep in front of relatives they can't stand in clothes they can't believe. As my readers will know, I'm a V.V. Romantik Soul, but this sounds like Torture to me. When Daniel and *Moi* plight our Troth, we shall exchange rings of hand carved wood, under a new moon Etck. If you aren't married, you can't get divorced. It's worked for my parents – or it would if they got on better . . .

Actually, this is a bit of an Achilles heel for *moi* as I wld secretly like my parents to be Married. It wld make me feel More Secure. This is an example of Double Standards. So much for The Aisle. See WEDDINGS.

Ask yourself: Do we share the same hobbies?

ANKLES

This is how my posh gran says 'uncle'. V. Confusing. E.g. "Shame your mother didn't marry your ankle" Etck.

Bits that join feet to legs. Once thought to be height of
eroticism, viz phrases like: 'well-turned ankles' Etck.
Nowadays, thanx to fashions designed by people like
moi, these are usually covered in four pairs of socks and
DMs the size of camels' feet. Boyz' ankles have, as far as
I know, never been a big focus of attraction, except on
Match of the Day when they writhe around inside the
penalty box clutching them, but if you are a genuine
Teenage Worrier, you may find yourself having a little
worry about your ankles. Viz: how would your life
change if you woke up one morning to find your ankles
had been turned for ever into Pink Marshmallows? This
kind of thing can make you ponder on just how
overlooked the significance of Ankles is. It can also
make you wonder if you've Gone Mad, so let's move
quickly on to . . .

ANNIVERSARY

A time of joy, celebration, memory of major event, like
when Granny Chubb takes three buses and a half-mile
walk to go to the V. Grotty cemetery where Grandad
Chubb is buried, every year on the anniversary of his
Banana. She always takes a single red rose, it is V.
Touching. Oh dear, I'm getting weepy now, but this
book is about LURVE, and the most Lurving
relationship I know is that of Granny and Grandpa

Chubb, which sadly is now over, doom, gloom, nothing lasts for ever Etck.

This is why we must grasp all opportunities for True LURVE with both hands (this is not a Naughty Bit, either, but From The Heart, not that some things can't be both).

Teenage Worriers shld celebrate as many Anniversaries as poss, 'cos we don't have enough parties.

Although I occasionally dream of D.H. behaving like this, my main response to the above is, puke

ANORAKS

If you wish to be LURVEd by anyone other than a
Train Spotter, Routemaster Bus Fan Club Organizer, or
Fell Walker, leave this item out of your wardrobe.
Reverse process if Train Spotters Etck are your personal
Cloud Nine candidates. Interestingly, V. Hip
streetwise up-yo-ass-type fashions are now moving
toward outer garments strangely similar to the Humble
Anorak, with hoods, bulgy low-slung pockets,
drawstrings Etck. There are however subtle differences
that distinguish the terminal Nerd from the Cutting
Edge, streetsmart, cash-economy, Urban Survivor and
in my part of London it isn't all that easy to know what
they all are. Just wearing a pair of Toys'Я'Us shades
with a purple Youth Hostelling number isn't enough,
however.

ANTICIPATION

'It's better to travel hopefully than to arrive.' This is a
clever way of saying that when you get something you
dream of, it doesn't always feel as good as you thought
it would, but 1) I know this will not happen re Daniel,
with whom the Earth Will Move Etck, and b) anyone
who says 'well why dunnee come back t'yer now then?'
does not have Poetry In Their Soul and therefore is not
a fit reader of this Great Work. I will not refund your
money however, as it is up to you to become a Better

Person, guided by this Helpful Tome, end of commercial break.

As a little kid, anticipation was about sweeties, Christmas, school hols Etck. As a big kid, it is still about these things but it quivers anew with the vibration of Cupid's bow . . . (quiver, quiver)

You are going to a Party. Will *he* be there?

He *is* there. Will he ask you *out*?

He does. Will you *kiss*?

You *do* kiss. Will he ask you out *again*? (yawn).

In fact, this is where it gets exciting . . . but just in case you missed the point, anticipation is always with us. It doesn't matter how many of life's ambitions you've achieved, there is still another Hope around the corner, other mountains to climb Etck Etck. It is V. Tiring, also V. Imp to remember how, as a little kid when you wanted Smarties you got Refreshers Etck. I asked for a lion suit every Christmas from the age of four until I was eleven. I wanted a V. Realistic one that I could frighten the neighbours with. That lion suit is still in my head, but that's the only place it ever was, and I think a Little Bit of Me Shrivelled Up when it never came.

APHRODISIACS

phew, cold shower...
LURVE POTION

LURVE potions made from ground rhino's horn (not OK re a threatened species), elixir of Oyster (Bad if allergic to seafood or sentimental re: Walrus and

Carpenter), or just bucketfuls of booze rendering beLURVed incapable of Knowing Own mind (also, in case of Boyz, knowing how to work Own Body). I am experimenting with ecologically sound, politically correct, legal LURVE potions but am beginning to wonder whether this is what is known as a Paradox. Please send Your Ideaz, recipes Etck to me c/o the Publisher.

ARMS

I do not like to add to the load of Worries you may already be bowed down by, but I am V.V. Worried

about my arms, as they are nearly as long as my legs.
Our ancient ancestors, as dug up by archaeologists
Etck, would have no trouble recognizing *moi* as a
member of their species and I always take a detour if in
the vicinity of apes, for fear they will get excited and
start showing me their bottoms. However, I saw a
pavement artist doing *Lion King* drawings with his feet
the other day, which made me think I shld be grateful
for the arms I've got, however daft.

LURVE your arms! (Ban other sorts, eg: superguns
Etck and, if two nations have a quarrel, just get oldest
members of both countries to biff each other until one
submits.)

L. Chubb slogan
no. 426 →

ARMS are for
CUDDLING
Not
FIGHTING

AUNTS

Like anoraks, aunts shld be banned from romantic
encounters. Specially the glam ones like the floozie my
Dear Mother cringingly calls her 'kid sister' who, when
she's whacked back a few Valpolicellas, is not a woman
I wld trust alone on the sofa with my LURVEd One, or
even myself for that matter. I realized this at the tender
age of 11, when I noticed her giving a V. Lingering
goodbye kiss to her sister's Significant Other – my
Dear Papa. Imagine, if she feels like this about my
emulsion-encrusted, panic-stricken aged relative, what
she wld do with a hunk like DH!!?

CHAPTER TWO
BBBBBBBEEEEZE

Just THREE weeks till half-term (tingle of lobes, trembling in every pore Etck). I am V.V. superstitious about giving any details of DHAM, but I can't resist telling you.

What happens is this. This is the kind of stuff that makes Machiavelli look like Mother Theresa.

*I go to the airport to wave Aggy off (her mother's fancy man is paying for the trip, much to the chagrin of Aggy's V. Nice, Caring, Sharing Dad). Aggy, of course, will be accompanied by **Daniel** who she will be hoping for a tearful farewell with. She will NOT be pleased to see moi, but I will be wearing distraught visage, painted-on tearstains Etck, thinly concealing A Great Sorrow.*

I will say a modest farewell to them, making light of my Distress, don't worry about me, it's nothing, just something at home, you have a great time Etck Etck. Then I will catch Daniel's sleeve as he turns to follow her and press a note into his hand with an imploring look.

The note will bear the simple leg end or legend:
'MUST KILL SELF. CAN WE TALK ONE LAST
TIME?'

Daniel will already be sodden with grief at the prospect of
a whole week without Aggy-poo, so his heartstrings will be
all the more vulnerable to vibrating when plucked by the
courageous battle against Tragedy being fought by moi . . .

When he comes back from seeing the plane off, things will
have got worse. I will now be limping glamorously, my leg
swathed in bandages. Trying to smile through my pain, I will
explain how, blinded by tears of sadness, I was run over by a
Haitian Airways trolley and have spent the last hour in First
Aid and no, I don't think anything is broken but nothing
matters now anyway, and gosh, how perfectly sweet *of him to*
offer to take me home and I couldn't possibly . . . (Spiggy
thinks I should choose this moment to faint, just in case he
doesn't offer, but I think that's a bit over the top) . . .
anyway, he will insist. When he does, I'll tell him I've heard
from the vet that Rover has to be put down due to a rare cat
illness, and that without her to curl up with at night, life is
a dessert, rice pudding for instance. Maybe if there was
Someone Special in my life, it would ease the pain. But there
isn't . . .

Swoon, violins, a whole week to persuade him of his terrible
mistake in turning my Lurve away. Reunion, moon-in-June,
swoon-to-our-tune, sigh, tremble, writhe, off-into-Sunset Etck
Etck.

I feel V. Cheerful now I have shared this with you. Must
make list for Big Day.

BIG DAY LIST ♡

1. **MAKE UP.** V. Imp to get flushed but natural look. ♡

2. **Big Roll BANDAGES.** ⟶♡→

3. **V. Big BAG** to conceal same.

4. **ANTISEPTIC.** Risky. But whiff of same shld convince D.H. I risked blood poisoning in the Temble Trolley Trauma.

5. **Big Prezzie** for Aggy-poo. (Nice touch, heh, heh)

6. **DOSH** (loads.. tubes, taxis Etck).

7. **Clothes** Arg. WHAT?! ♡

I bet Tolstoy, Jeffrey Archer Etck never had to keep hiding their Great Works under the pillow when their mothers swan in not respecting their privacy Etck. I have just retrieved this Great Work from under same as my adored Mother came in looking for her bra (I know I shouldn't have borrowed it but I am engaged in major engineering experiment with wires and *padding that makes the Channel Tunnel project look like excavating a boiled egg).*

V. Ashamed to admit that I am extracting some of the dosh that I put into the Granny Chubb Specs Endeavour (GCSE) to support DHAM, but this is the only way money works in The City, and you have to invest to expand Etck. Slight problems re mechanism of Benjy's Tyrannosaurus money-box. To get money out you have to shoot it between the eyes with Hi-Velocity Telescopic Dino-Blasting springloaded dart gun, at which it falls over with legs in the air and money is expelled from its bum with gross realistic noise, yeech. Tyrannosaurus not co-operating, despite direct hits. Must try alternative methods.

V. Worried about Rover, whose mangy patch is two mm bigger than last month, particularly now that I'm taking her name in vain as central alibi in DHAM. V.V.V.V.V. Worried about my Father, who said he was 'too low' even to play Dolphs. Does he mean too short, or too depressed?? V.V.V.V.V.V.V.V. Worried about my mother, who definitely overreacted to the bra situation. I've no **idea** how it found its way into Horace's cage. Can Horace be a cross-dresser? Of course I got the blame. Offices could hire gerbils as paper-shredders and save fossil fules. Anyway, my mother thinks I should PAY her for it. Where does she think a penniless teenager is going to get the dosh?? I must struggle to think of higher things and proceed with the BEEEEEEEEEEEEEEEEZE.

SOCIAL INSECURITY in the caring 90s...
NB: 'Designer Kid' does not mean yr offspring will
excel at computer graphics

BABIES

One far distant day, you may want LURVE's sublime
pashiones to result in the next generation of Teenage
Worriers. If you want them now, however, I wld ask a
frend to send for men in White coats to cart you off for
suitable period (ie: until you can earn living, pat baby's
head and rub its tummy at same time, warm up milk
without incinerating self Etck). Sadly, Community
Care has led to V. Little provision in the men in White
coats dept, so you are more likely to be cast pregnant
into snow. Arg, moan, contraception Etck. V. Unfair
that us gurlz are now supposed to bake our own bread,
run for parliament and have a couple of designer
kiddies too.

    See PREGNANCY.

BANTER

Cheery backchat designed to woo beLURVEd and show them you are not just a pretty face, or *even* a pretty face, in the sad case of *moi*. It is V. Discouraging for heterosexual female Teen Worriers to discover that although a sense of Humour is V. Imp to them, Boyz often see it differently.

When a boy, frinstance, says a girl has a V. Good sense of Humour, he usually means she laughs at his

terrible jokes, ie: 'If I said you had a lovely body, would you hold it against me?' Etck. But here followeth the L.Chubb Humour Tips Dept:

1) Do not give in to temptation to fall over and wiggle your legs in the air at his jokes UNLESS they are funny. Just like with stupid presents you never wanted from relatives, if you look too keen you'll just get more and more of the same. Also, coolness is Attraktive (so I'm told, it's never worked for me, but then neither has Enthusiasm either, moan whinge).

2) Make a joke and test his reaction. If joke not funny and he laughs, this means he likes you V.V.V. Much and is trying to please you. If joke is funny and he throws you pained, patronising look, then ask yourself, a) is he jealous of yr scintillating wit, or b) does he just not have a sense of humour? Either is not

promising. True banter, dear reader(s), depends on a meeting of like minds, twin souls in flight Etck, exchanging repartee with speed of light in true communion of Equals.

I practise banter in front of a mirror three or four times a day and I think in a few years I will be ready to try it out on a real live boy. Not that I'll need to, luckily, as I will by then be in my cozy nest with Daniel (swooooon), but I know that some of you sadly will not be so lucky.

BASTARD

V. Insulting and abusive term still often used (esp in macho Brit army and cop shows, viz: the standard, Step One 'you BASTARD!' or the more subtle, male-bonding 'you're a mean BASTARD', or in anxious middle-class marriage-on-rocks dramas, viz: 'It's taken me all these years to see what a BASTARD you really are' Etck). Use now pretty out of date, because a V. Large number of V. Nice people (like *moi*, frinstance) really are BASTARDS because it only means your parents are not married (at least, not to each other).
   CAMPAIGN TO MAKE BASTARD A NICE WORD, viz: 'In recognition of Your services to the community, I hereby Knight you with the Royal order of the Bastard' Etck.

BEACH

Strong associations with LURVE, entwined amid lapping blue waters Etck. English beaches not suitable, re pebbles, foul sewer outfalls, barnacled breakwaters, icy waves the colour of Granny Chubb's raincoat. Since I am built like a paperclip, the Beach is not one of my preferred settings. However, the Brit climate can prove to be a positive advantage bodywise, as it gives an opportunity to wrap up and yet still have the romantic sound of waves crashing about, seagulls squawking, wind howling. You HAVE to cuddle up to somebody in this Living Hell scenario.

Beaches are however V. Good spots for the exchange of romantic gifts, eg: pebbles shaped like hearts (paint them with your initials, or just leave them natural), driftwood you can make into mobiles, picture frames Etck (maybe I cld get a job on the Craft Page of *Housewives Weekly*). Personally, I wld like a stick of rock with Daniel's name all the way through it (sigh). I foolishly mentioned this to Hazel once, who made a V. Rude joke about it. Just the same, we both concluded that this is probably a cosmetic operation Boyz will soon be able to have.

See also HOLIDAYS.

BEAST

If beasts looked like this, it would be easy to avoid them. Sadly, they often look V. Nice.

There is a V. Widely held misconception that we Gurlz

like a bloke who is a bit of a Beast Viz: *Beauty and the Beast* and other stories of maidens in thrall to ogres Etck. Boyz also like to support this view, either because they are Beasts and want to Control Your Life, or because they aren't but would like to be.

An old friend of my mother's is married to an alcoholic. He doesn't beat her up, but he shouts at her all day and night. Both their kids left home at 16, but she stays. Then there's Josie, in the lower sixth. She was 7 when her Mum fled to a battered wives' refuge and Josie is still terrified her dad will find them. Then there's Misha, who used to come to school covered in bruises and her mum said she kept falling downstairs. It took a V. long time for the social services to cotton on to the fact that the bruises came from her dad, who fractured her skull in the end. These are the worst things that can happen if people think it's normal for Boyz to be Beasts. Often these Boyz were abused by their parents too, and need treatment themselves and don't know it.

HOW TO SPOT BEASTS AND BULLIES

1) If a boy hurts you, go. If he's done it once, he'll do it again and if you marry him, he'll do it regularly.

2) Be V. Suspicious of any Boy who thinks stories of cruelty are funny. One of the Yorkshire Ripper's mates didn't report him for going after a woman with rocks because he thought it was Just One Of Those Things, maybe even A Bit Of A Laugh.

3) Be V. Suspicious of a boy who calls women or

Gurlz Slags, or Slappers. It usually means he doesn't like *any* women V. much.

4) Beware of thinking these kind of blokes will be different with you and that somehow you can change them. There are plenty of V. Nice boyz around who don't behave like this so why make a martyr of yourself and wreck your own life trying to make a Beast into a Prince? Disneyworld is OK in the Cinema, but shld not Guide Yr Life.

BEAUTY

In eye of beholder Etck; see also LOOKS.

Here's a V. Touching story about my New Frend Spiggy, who is not at all superficial, but like all us humans, is susceptible to the byooooty of the human form. She got a crush on a small, dark Maltese boy when she was 13. But her head was also turned by his Best Friend, who made Apollo look like Kermit The Frog. One day she followed her Malteser and the God down the street together. One was tall and golden, the other bandy-legged and scruffy, with shoulders like ski-slopes . . . and she felt overwhelming LURVE. Not for the God, but for the Malteser.

Spiggy and her Malteser write to each other every day, an example of Lurve transcending distance, and a beautiful example of Beauty itself being discerned in the humble wayside tumbleweed rather than the extravagant blooming rose. I rely on this when I think

Lurve Objects: The Fantasy...

... what's available Locally

that it's possible for DH to LURVE me despite my, er, shortcomings, weediness, spots, knobbly bits Etck.

The ridiculous thing about beauty is that *no-one* ever thinks they actually possess it, not even Hazel, who has quadruple the amount of this elusive quality dished out to her than *moi*, and still moans about not being able to do a thing with the tawny silken waterfall of wig that nature gave her such a generous dollop of. It's enough to make you throw up.

At the other end of the scale is Aggy, who cld certainly do with a few beauty tips, what with her pebble lenses and complexion like a brillo pad, but yet she swans off with handsomest Boy in World (ie: Daniel Hope). This is terrible for *moi*, but proves Looks Aren't Everything. Grrr.

BED

spring has sprung

Lurve within the Holy Writ of Marriage between two consenting adults (er, my publisher insists that since this is a family book that may get into school libraries Etck, I must include important moral sentiments like this . . . and of course I totally agree, ahem) leads eventually away from the thrashing about in the back row of the cinema, school bike-shed, writhing mass of limbs, tongues and socks at party Etck, to the clean, sweet-smelling, freshly laundered sheets of the Honeymoon suite.

Pile of rose petals in meadow
(take hot water bottle plus thermos)

Make LURVE in a bath of asses' milk...

Or your parents' bed (not in my case, sob)

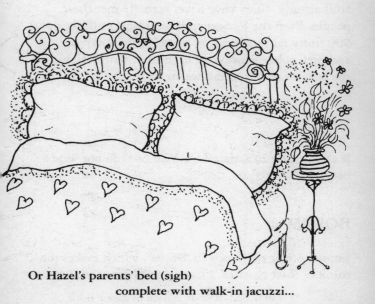

Or Hazel's parents' bed (sigh)
        complete with walk-in jacuzzi...

Writing about beds has made me feel a bit sad as I am sure I will never get into bed with the Boy of my Dreamz and also, I do not want a double bed anyway as it will mean giving up my bedhead with the picture of ickle lambs on that I have had since I was 7. This is V. Insecure and weedy of me I know but despite V. Big Hormonal Urges, molten spasms that engulf my very being Etck, I sometimes wish I was 7 again and sitting on Granny Chubb's knee with my teddy. (Wld Daniel let me take my teddy to bed, I wonder? If not, he is not the man for me.)

I expect sophisticated Teen Worriers will have thrown this book away by now, having done all this stuff already. But I have never actually met these people. Even the V. Sexperienced Hazel still has about 900 fluffy rabbits hanging from her bedroom ceiling and prefers her winceyette nightshirt with bunnies on the bosoms to red satin sheaths Etck.

BEIGE

If attempting to attract LURVEd one, do not wear beige.

BOSOM

I much prefer this word to 'Breast', which makes me think of roast chicken. I have already bemoaned my lack of a pneumatic figure at length and I am V. Sorry to report that the last few months have seen no change in the L. Chubb Bosom Dept, all contributions gratefully received Etck. In fact, I think my pining has led to a V. Small deflation. Although I measure my bust every two days (I am V. Proud of getting down to this, as I used to measure it three times daily, especially when I was using the wonderexpander kit I sent off for in *Smirk* magazine), I am still uncertain of its exact

measurement as I sometimes have three or four jumpers on in the winter when my Adored Father is Fixing the Central Heating (this operation lasts all winter and is finished when the first crocuses appear) which makes my winter measurements much bigger than my summer ones. One day I will summon up the courage to Face the Ghastly Truth and measure myself in my nakedity. But I know myself well enough, dear reader, to realize I must choose the psychological moment with Care, ie: when I am firmly ensconced in a Long Term relationship with a Certain Person who will LURVE me for myself alone and not for such V. Unimportant things as the size of my bits.

Big bras, cleavages Etck are currently making a comeback, bulging all over the hoardings Etck. Whatever happened to feminism moans my ancient mother, and, while I would not have been seen dead in some of the things politically correct people wore in the 1970s, I agree just the same. There is little doubt in my mind that if blokes had to wear little straps round their willies to hold them pointing up so everyone could stare at them, more Boyz wld complain about Oppression, Sexism, Etck. (Some might find their LURVE lives improving overnight, but since they must hang out, as it were, with V. Shallow people, we can draw a veil over them, and not a moment before time too, phew.)

I must spare a thought for those of you who feel V. Embarrassed to have a V.V. Big Bosom. It must be V. Annoying when Boyz pretend to be engaging in soulful conversation re Plato, Milton, *Neighbours* Etck whilst never raising their eyeline above yr chest. Big Bertha (who left Sluggs comp last year in a cloud of glory being the first student to get more than six GCSEs) used to actually put real balloons under her jumper sometimes and then POP them when she got this sort of treatment.

What is V. daft is that it is exactly the same boyz who josh V. crude remarks about bazooms as who moan, faint, puke Etck when they see the perfectly normal activity of breastfeeding, which of course is what bosoms were put on the planet to do.

CAMPAIGN FOR PUBIC (sorry, public) BREASTFEEDING NOW!

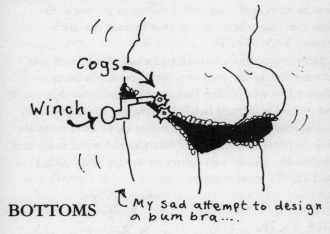

My sad attempt to design a bum bra....

BOTTOMS

Bottoms are a different matter from bosoms altogether, as they are of equal and absolute importance to both genders and um, their main uses are for other books than this to deal with (see Medical encyclopaedia if in doubt). All gurlz know that a pert, wedge-shaped bottom is what to aim for, but although I have spent many tortured hours at my drawing board I have been unable to devise a bum-bra that does not leave a visible line. Teenage Think Tank Members shld work hard on this and send me their designs ASAP so that I can patent them and we can all make V. Big dosh and of course be useful to the community.

Notice that I am much less censorious about the Bottom than I am about Bazooms. This is because the first thing I noticed about Daniel was his exceptionally slim, yet subtly curved posterior, and also because my own bottom is V. neat and I therefore do not suffer from the Pear phenomenon that haunts the 20th century Teen Worrier.

However, I must not adopt Double Standards just because this is one area in which I have not been blighted by Malignant Fate, and of course while a small and perfectly formed behind is fine behind a boy, it is V. Useless for a gurl, who is supposed to have cellulite Etck to protect her and her infants. So I have, sadly and reluctantly, decided to subscribe to the BAN SEXY BOTTOMS movement also.

BREAKING UP

Sadly, part of LURVE is its ending. It is V. diff to end a relationship when you have decided to do it. But it is V. Much worse when you haven't. So the most pukesome thing you can say if you've decided to leave someone, is that it hurts you more than them, which is a V. Big Lie. Teen Worriers, however, are not usually seeking advice about how to leave someone, but rather how to get someone back, or survive without them.

Symptoms of being left range from Mooning around playing V. Old records, hugging sleeve of jumper beLURVEd left behind, weeping copiously over V. bad photo booth snapshot of BeLURVEd, writing V. Long poems, writing even longer letters, tearing letters up, sitting by phone knowing there has been a dreadful mistake and LURVEr will call any moment to Right the Wrong.

L. Chubb's Tips for DEALING WITH LEAVING (read this to accompaniment of wailing of violins, melancholy cry of banshee, tapes of worshippers at Wailing Wall, rustle of Kleenex Etck):

1) Initially, resist all advice to get LURVEd one back. If they want to return, they will. (NB I know I am excepting myself from this rule, but it is only because these are the V. Special circs of Real True LURVE in which my LURVEd one was Stole From Me, and anyway, I have waited several weeks before pursuing him.)

2) Play V. Sad music V. Loud as you slowly tear up all mementoes of LURVEd one. Put these on bonfire (not in your room). On second thoughts, save one photo to show your grandchildren and remind you of Lucky Escape. (Also, just in case he turns out to be their Grandfather as you went a bit further than you meant and the condom broke.)

3) Do Not speak to anyone who tells you you've had a lucky escape or that Your LURVEd One is a Worm, has brain of amoeba Etck. By suggesting you cld have

LURVEd a worm all along, it is V. Patronising, or Matronising depending on who's saying it.

4) Avoid places you went together. This is V. Difficult if you are at the same school, or if Your LURVEd One is the sibling of your Best Friend, in which case follow Tip 5, below. In most cases, however, you will not appreciate your Special Song, Special Caff, Special Paving stone Etck without yr beLURVEd at your side. Until I am reunited with Daniel, I will always avoid the postbox in which I posted him my letters.

5) BUT if your beLURVEd is a schoolmate, or Best Frend'z sibling, then your only alternative is to WALLOW. This means you cry as loudly at your desk or in your BF's bedroom, as you possibly can. This is V.V. Embarrassing for the LURVE Object and will teach him or her to be more careful next time.

6) After initial lengthy period of deep mourning, weeping, talking on phone to your friend (unless as in my case she Stole Your Man) Etck you are ready to move into Phase Two, which is Getting-Out-and-About. Do something New And Challenging like training to be an astronaut, pursuing higher Mathematics Etck. Or you could take up volleyball (pretend his head is the ball) or playing violin (make sure you go for jolly fiddler's tunes, otherwise mournful sound will induce nostalgia). Er, as you see, my own list keeps reminding *moi* of LURVE, but then I am a Teenager Obsessed . . .

DO NOT...

A) Wander through Autumn leaves smelling bonfire smoke...

B) Play your father's copy of the Righteous Brothers singing 'you've Lost that Loving Feeling'.

c) Read LURVE poetry.

d) Go to soppy films ← Even taking Benjy to 'The Lion King' induced grief in Moi. Lion V.V. like Daniel.

e) WONDER what you will DO in Summer, next Christmas, your birthday Etck.

F) Watch SOAPS. You will only think how V.V. superficial they are and how they never deal with a HEART THAT IS TRULY BROKEN, like yours....

All the above will only induce Pining...

DO...

A). Keep **BIG DIARY** of how you feel...
This will one day be source of great
mirth, esp to younger sibling...

b). **Padlock & hide Diary.**

c). Read **Great Novels**. These show how it
has all happened before, so you feel less
alone...

D.) Make list of **Belurved's good** &
bad points, each Sunday. After 3
months the **good** list will be shorter,
the **bad** much longer. When **Bad**
list (which prob started as a blank
page) has overtaken **Good** list, you
are **CURED.** ← NB Also remember, main
bad point is that this person
did not return yr LURVE.
They did not recognise
True Byooty of yr Soul
and are therefore Not
worthy...

CHAPTER THREE
CCCCCCEEEEEEEEEEZZZZE
and DDDDDDS

*The worst thing in the world has happened. If I was Sherlock
Holmes, or Spiggy had even half the brain of Doctor Watson,
we would never have let such an obvious fact escape us.*

Glume, grue Etck.

*We never checked whether Daniel was accompanying Aggy
to the airport!*

*And in the midst of a casual chat with Aggy (to check out
the fine details of our Master Plan, like when the plane was
going, which airport, Etck), Aggy pointed out that he can't
come to see her off because he has a different Half-term! Well
of course he does, being at the Nobs Academy for Lord
Fauntleroy and Co rather than at Humble Sluggs
Comprehensive for Proles, like us.*

*All this passes Spiggy by, as being from a nation inhabited
only by upside-down convicts, she has no understanding of the
great Brit Class System. Gnash, gnash, rent of garments,
howling of coyotes, dingos Etck.*

*Now I will never find an excuse to get Daniel on his own.
I must consign my hopes to the Dustbin of Dreams Etck. I
have put all my DHAM dosh into GCSE Tyrannosaurus
Guilt-Edged Security Box now, and if it won't let me have it
back that's all the bigger obstacle to temptation until the
magic Granny Chubb's Specs total is reached, at which point
I can open it with one of my adored Father's power tools and*

buy Benjy off with a V. Small amount of the proceeds.
  Alas. And woe.

STOP PRESS STOP PRESS
  Aggy has just called round to say Daniel has got leave to get off early on Fri after all!
  She is Over the Moon and so am I (wild cackle, Special EFX Dept of hands rubbing together, cauldrons bubbling Etck). How soon are the bat's wings of despair turned into the softly beating cherubs' pinions of Hope! How soon does the plummeting plunge into the chasm of Despondency transform into the soaring arc of buoyant optimism and renewed, um, joie de vivre (must practise that French tape for my weekend in Paris with DH — we'll go by boat, or maybe chunnel — flying still makes me feel I'd rather go over Niagara Falls in a barrel full of jellyfish).
  But how to quell the mad cackling Doshiverous Tyrannosaurus Glasses for Granny Chubb monster and get the money out? To soothe myself, I will get on with the CCCCEEEEEEZZE . . .

CANOODLE

My Dictionary defines this V. Pleasant word as 'to cuddle amorously, fondle . . .' It always makes me think of doves, small fluffy creatures Etck rather than gleaming sweaty bits heaving about on red satin sheets, but Romance is a V. Imp part of LURVE, and Canoodling a V. Imp part of Romance. Teenage LURVErs canoodle at every opportunity, ie: under school desks, on tops of buses Etck, often grumbled at by ancient disapproving Persons who've forgotten, or never knew, that when Canoodling with that Special Person, you forget anyone else is there. It can be V. Upsetting, when you are without a canoodling partner, to see that everyone else is canoodling, but L. Chubb's advice is to smile serenely and think, 'My time will come'.

CARDIGAN

Avoid this item of clothing. See ANORAK.

CAT

'Small, furry, domesticated, carnivorous, quadruped.' How little these words convey! How limited is the

Rover querying her dictionary
definition...

language of the dictionary to describe the adorable
attributes of Rover! One might as well describe Daniel
Hope as a tall, smooth, undomesticated, omniverous
biped.

See PETS for more on the LURVE of a good animal.

CHESS

L. Chubb's advice to clever Teenage Worriers is, if you
want to Impress the Boy or Girl of Your Dreams, Take
up Chess. It is a V. Excellent opportunity for late night
liaisons as it is a *game only two can play*. And, since the
object of the game is to Mate your opponent, there are
opportunities for sharing rude jokes Etck in games

between LURVErs that don't look very likely when you just see two frowning, mad-looking blokes in sports jackets playing it on TV.

Daniel is the top chess player in his school and the thought of him and Aggy in mental combat over the board has made me V. Interested in this noble game. I am learning the pawn's move and it is times like this when I wish I was V.V.V.V. Brainy like Aggy or else had gone to a posh school with chess clubs Etck instead of media studies.

CINEMA

Many a LURVE has blossomed in the back row. If the only choice of film is *Laserman, Serial Killer III* Etck, so much the better, 'cos then you can Canoodle (see CANOODLE) all over the back seats without bothering to watch. Although even the proximity of Daniel could not prevent me from gluing my eyes to *101 Dalmatians,* probably the greatest Film ever Made.

The movies are an essential tool with which to prove your Intellectual prowess to your beLURVEd, however. Here are some names you *need to know* to get on in the high-flying world of Movie Buff (or Movie Bluff):

1) Quentin Tarantino

This is the V. Hot Ticket New Director who has people splashing about in blood all over the place. These kinds of movie directors believe we are in an Age

Reservoir Bloggs

Of Action and Reaction, not Contemplation, so people keep bouncing from one thing to another like pinballs, which is probably why they get killed so often. Sadly, all his films are 18s, but you can live in hope (family book Etck).

2) **Casablanca**

This is a V. Old black and white LURVE movie featuring Humphrey Bogart and Ingrid Bergman in V. Fetching Hats. My dad V. Occasionally says things like 'here's looking at you, kid' and 'the lives of two little people don't amount to a hill of beans in this crazy world' to my adored mother when he has V. Hazy Distant Memory that he once won her heart by Wit, Charm Etck but she now takes as much notice as if he were the speaking clock.

3) **The Graduate**

Another oldie but goodie, about LURVE defeating forces of Oppression, Bourge Values, withered hand of bitter parents clutching at winged heels of Teenage LURVErs Etck. All Boyz who see this, dream of their

Frendz' mums turning into Anne Bancroft and hauling them off to hotels Etck, but are defeated by irrefutable evidence of runny make-up, torn tights, stringy hair, black-rimmed eyes, hangovers, smokers' coughs Etck among possible candidates. Maybe at posher school than Sluggs Comp the mums wld look more like Anne Bancroft.

NB L. Chubb's list of other 'must-see' Movies: *Les Enfants du Paradis, Wings of Desire, Solaris, West Side Story, The Commitments, The Piano. Naturellement*, you will soon be able to add the works of famed director L. Chubb to this list: soul-searching romances, cutting edge documentaries exposing corruption of World, as well as blockbusting adventure movies to rival Spielberg and make lotsa dosh, I mean improve our cultural heritage. Even Benjy complains that the only Brit SuperHero is Peter Pan and Spielberg even nicked him, just as Walt Disney nicked Pooh Bear and Alice in Wonderland.

CLITORIS

V. Important item situated just at front of Gurlz' vaginas sometimes known V. coyly as Love Button, which may explain why Hazel says some Boyz just press and hope somebody comes (ha ha). Just as Boyz' strongest sexual passions are centred on the willy, so Gurlz' are centred on the clitoris, and if you don't know where it is, you are going to have a hard time enjoying the many varieties of LURVEmaking that you can do without having sexual intercourse.

Gentle rubbing of the clitoris produces juices, and the juices it produces (NB must consider career as songwriter some time) lubricates yr Bits and makes it more fun for you and/or the entry of the Boy'z Willy (or Penis, if you want to be proper). Then (phew, cold shower, family book Etck) all these nice feelings get stronger and stronger until you achieve orgasm. If you practise by yourself you will get to understand how yr Own works, then you can show the person of your dreams what to do.

It is only quite recently that Girls' Strong Urges have been freely written and talked about, and many

O clitoris! Is an anagram of Solicitor!

But will such dazzling insights endear me to the Law Society?

generations of women weren't told about, or didn't even discover, their clitoris, and thought they were supposed to have a fantastic time from just Boyz being generous enough to Do It with them, no Foreplay or anything. This led to women doing lots of sighing, groaning Etck while thinking, 'Would it seem rude if I got up now to put the kettle on?'

There is a limit to openness, by the way. Hazel's neighbours, the 'bohemian' Plunket-Breezes, used to boast that they helped their daughter to examine her clitoris when she was 6! They told this story at dinner parties! Poor Virginia Plunket-Breeze was called Vagina Plunket-Breeze so often they had to change her name to Mary. She left home at 16 to do business studies.

COITUS INTERRUPTUS

Latin for yr Mother coming in with a cup of tea while you're Doing It.

Actually, people have used this method (known as withdrawal, viz Boyz pulling out before they come) as a form of contraception, but it is not to be recommended, because even the minutest drop of sperm can produce a baby, which may be a comfort to the boy in the fifth year examining the stuff under his microscope but not to Gurlz who don't yet want to hear the charming sounds of an ickle baba upstairs, wailing, yelling, cursing, puking Etck.

COME

See ORGASM, but this word also sometimes means sperm.

CONTRACEPTIVES

When LURVE approaches its climax and you are seething in surprising circumstances, it is not the best time to think: 'Has he got a condom?', or: 'Am I on the pill?' or: 'Is this how you really do it then? I always thought you had to stand on your head and wear frogman's flippers.' Forewarned is forearmed, dear reader(s) and it is best to discover contraception before the lack of it discovers you measuring out powdered milk and wondering where your youth has gone (probably to his mother, ha ha yeech).

Contraception is anything that stops the Boy'z sperm from fertilizing the Gurl'z egg, by which I do not mean that which comes out of a box marked 'Free Range' but the ones we clever Gurlz produce inside the Bod without even thinking about it. Many

Contraceptives are of the Barrier kind. This cld possibly include the bedroom wall with yr LURVEd one passionately calling yr name from the next room, but even in the age of Safe Sex is carrying safety a bit far. Barrier contraceptives are more usually the Condom (Sheath, rubber, french letter, johnny, willy cover) and the Cap. The Condom is a kind of thin rubber sock that Boyz pull over the Erection before getting anywhere near Yr Bits to catch the poor little hopeful Sperms in, and the Cap, as worn by the Female Person, is a BR ticket collector's with plastic reindeer antlers stapled on, which prevents conception by reducing Male Person to helpless hysterics on floor.

Actually, I was misinformed re that last bit, sorry. The Cap is, of course, a thin rubber diaphragm carefully inserted by the Gurlz to cover the neck of the Womb inside the Vagina, and accompanied by lashings of spermicidal cream Etck. There is also the new female condom or whatever it's called, the thing that goes inside The Bits like an even bigger sock, and which Rustles whilst Doing It (so I hear).

The Pill (which, if you get it from your doctor, you have to remember to take daily), the IUD (or coil, which is an intra-uterine device that the doc has to insert) and er, Not Doing It (my own contraceptive so far, whinge, moan) are all forms of contraception that, if used correctly, should prevent you from experiencing the joys of parenthood before your time.

But for Safer Sex (ie: intercourse that reduces risk of AIDS and other Sexually Transmitted Diseases or STDs) a condom is still the best protection. Always use

with water-based spermicide and don't put two condoms on at once, mistakenly thinking it's safer. Seems good wheeze I know, but one can break the other qu easily. *Moi*, I disguised myself as a 16-year-old and booked in at a strange doctor's when I was 12 to get contraceptive device (I mean, advice). I got some V. Funny looks from the receptionist (I suppose it was the leopardskin leggings and the wig) but I also got V.

It is no longer embarrassing to seek contraceptive
advice. I find shades & a trench coat adequate,
though many still prefer a paper bag over the head

Good advice and have carried a pack of three ever since (renewed every three months in case sell-by date approaches).

The doc said it is V. Imp to discover which is the best contraception for you, as some gurlz shld not use the Pill which also does not protect against STDs. He also pointed out that although we gurlz produce one egg a month, there are 100,000,000 sperms contained in the average ejaculation from a boy'z willy and it only takes one little spermlet to fertilize an egg arg. Any of you considering using the rhythm method (ie: only Doing It during infertile periods) or the withdrawal method (see COITUS INTERRUPTUS) might bear in

NB: You do not have to be Musical to use this method, but you do need thermometers, charts, a stable relationship

mind that sperm can leak out even when the boy does not come. And although a gurl'z most fertile time is exactly in between her periods, when she is ovulating (ie: producing the egg) it is V. Hard to tell when that time is. Also, spermlets can live inside you for up to three days.

All of which V. Worrying info only goes to prove L. Chubb's theory that Doing all sorts of other Juicy bits but stopping short of actual Doing It is the safest course of Action (as if some of us had any choice in the matter, moan, whinge, chance would be a fine thing Etck).

See phone numbers at end of buke.

CRUSHES
(Blushes)

V. Secret Anecdote....
I am V. SHY of telling you
this — but here goes....

The lofty insights of a 15-year-old (ahem) can look back on all the daft crushes of yoof (Brad Pittbull Etck, blush) and discern them from True Lerve. But while in their grip, it is V. hard to discern infatuation with soap stars, footballers, teachers Etck from the Real Thing. Here's a Sad Moral Tale, dear reader, that happened to *moi* (and which I haven't told anyone ever before — hold on to edge of seat, get Kleenex, pin back ears).

When I was an innocent 13-year-old I had a mega-crush on a supply teacher called Ken (LURVE can blind you to any imperfection). It was torture exposing my knobbly frame to him during PE lessons, but in an attempt to rouse him to a Fever I thrust a heaving 20 pages (or heaved a thrusting 20 pages, ha ha, yeech) of Purple Prose into his unsuspecting hands pretending it was an essay on the Life Cycle of the Wood Louse.

Anyway, I concluded he was a Wood Louse himself when he avoided my eyes for two weeks of broken nights, sodden pillows Etck, and then he eventually asked me to come to the Staffroom after school. Joy, Heaven on Earth Etck! I realized he had just been Shy and that we would consume our Passion (I think it's consummated, but consume sounds, well, *hungrier*) there and then on the coffee-stained carpet amid the trodden-in dog-ends Etck. I spent my dinner money on a pack of three Hot Dog ketchup-flavoured condoms by sneaking into the men's loo next to the Dog and Duck car park, which I was still clutching hotly in my hand when the staffroom door was opened by a smiling Ms Wright, the Fourth Years' teacher who was waiting in there with him.

Aaaargh!

He had asked her to come, he said, because he had not wanted there to be a misunderstanding and he thought she might be able to Offer Me Support that he could not. The Pain Of It! I was so embarrassed I dropped the condoms on the floor and Ken picked them up and then gave Ms Wright a look that seemed to say a) this person is too pathetic and deluded to live, and b) these look better than the ones we used last night. I might have imagined the last bit, but you do in situations like this.

They told me I was still a child, and there was much in childhood to be enjoyed for as long as possible. Yuk. I exclaimed furiously that I was not, but unfortunately the wild waving of my apology for arms resulted in a cascade of old brushes and several gallons of paint water materializing from the shelf above, covering him, me, Ms Wright and most of the staffroom floor, and proving his point. He returned my now damp 20 page LURVE letter, saying that he had read only two lines and that he felt it was better not to read the rest, and I knew LURVE between us was an Impossible Dream. This is what happens if you get Out of Order with teachers.

I should add that age and hindsight have showed me how lucky I was that Ken didn't take advantage of my yoof and innocence however, as I am reliably formed that some V. Seedy teachers do . . .

See also GROUPIES.

CUPID

Small fat God of Love who looks V. like my ickle brother, even down to bow and arrow. Sometimes known as Eros, although the V. Famous statue of Eros in pcc Circus was meant by the sculptor to be a figure of Charity, not Lurve. Disappointing to all LURVErs who conjugate, I mean, congregate there, but I must speak True. If Cupid's arrow pierces you, you fall in love with next living thing you see.

Benjy has never forgiven my mother for dressing
him up as Cupid when he was four

DDDDDDDDDDDDDDDDDS

DANCING

Old-fashioned dances like the Tango are coming back,
I hear. This is V. Good news for fit agile Teen Worriers
as the Tango originally meant Doing It. Not V. Good
news for *moi*, however, as glass ankles and unruly pipe-
cleaner style limbs make L. Chubb's attempts to glide
sinuously round a dance floor look like a grisly
postmodern ballet for the UnDead. Rave type gyrations
are no good for LURVers, however, being lonesome
journeys of the Soul. Bring back the Smooch, says El
Chubb, where you can drape yourself sinuously round
beLURVed and let him do the moving. Langwid. Etck.

DENIM

V. Sexy material when worn with metal fly buttons, no
hips, bare feet Etck by DH. (Swoon, sigh, cold shower
Etck.)

DIARY

Essential Item for all Teenage Worriers in LURVE, but
must be kept under padlock and key. The most famous

OCTOBER

25 SUNDAY

22nd after Trinity

Boring day. Cry a bit.

26 MONDAY

School. Grooh.

P.E. grone.

27 TUESDAY

School again. YUK.

28 WEDNESDAY

More school.

NB: This V. unedifying e.g. of my diary last year is an object lesson in how NOT to enter ye portals of posterity (Doodle by Benjy)

Diaries (like Samuel Pepys') were read by Posterity, which means people who came after them. I'd like to give Posterity a laugh as much as the next person, but I find it hard to imagine Teenage Worriers in the year 4000 finding my anguish about bras Etck V. Stimulating.

Anyway, main advice for a diary. Write in it things you wld not dare say to anyone else. Don't give up on it. It is amazing how often I have wished I had kept writing in my diary. I wish frinstance I cld look back in close detail on the crush I had on that Teacher. Already the mists of time are dimming his unforgettable words and it might give me strength to know the future is not All bad, as at the time, I knew I would never, ever, LERVE another but Him.

V. IMP DIARY TIP:

Be sure to write this at the beginning of your diary: *'This diary is entirely a work of fiction and bears no relation to my actual life as it is lived. Anything I say about adults (who may have similar names to my parents) or peers (who may have similar names to my frendz) or younger people (who may have similar names to my siblings) is entirely a figment of my imagination.'*

DIET

← Remember.
"One Fudge a day
keeps glume at bay"

I am V.V.V.V. FED UP with articles in *Smirk, Weenybop, TruLuv, Yoohoo!* Etck Etck telling us to eat

campaign for Real Fudge

properly and badgering us to be thin. Any plump Teen Worriers out there, this is not because I am lank, attenuated, flimsy, puny, meagre Etck myself, but because I am V.V. Sad that Greedy Editors, Diet Manufacturers Etck and anorexic, terminally depressed superwaifs are raking in vast amounts of dosh to make us Feel Bad and spend our cash on their trash. Teenage-Worriers-in-LURVE are the most vulnerable victims of this mean old exploitative rubbish, but believe me, diets DON'T WORK. If you eat V. Little, your body stores every spare calorie, and the minute you eat normally again, you get fat. On top of that, if you think about your weight all the time, it just makes you V. Miserable, like the 39%(!) of 12-13 yr old Gurlz who want to lose weight in this country! That's well over a third!

It's V. Imp to remember that models are the ones out of step, not everybody else. Most models are size 10 or 12, but the av size for Brit Female Persons is 16. ie: viz, not only are most people not like models, but most people will become LURVE partners of people not like models, including those Boyz you know whose tongues hit the floor when they see the Gurlz in magazines.

There is a fast food chain in Los Angeles called 'Fatburger' which has opened nine new restaurants in the last couple of years. Meanwhile a major weight loss empire has closed 30 centres! So maybe these Crucial Truths are getting through. As long as you eat some fresh veg, fruit, carbohydrate, protein and fat (yes! fat! cod liver oil capsules V. good for you) each day and walk to school Etck you will be V. healthy and a normalish weight. I like my veg with fudge, but we all have our peculiarities.

Here is a sample of Benjy's diet for one day, as noted down in L. Chubb's Diary:

<u>Breakfast</u>: Large bowl of *Fabbogems* + milk. *Fabbogems* are a mix of cereal and little brightly coloured marshmallows shaped as goblins, teddies or space vehicles. Benjy refuses to eat the teddies (soft-hearted) or the space vehicles (which he collects). He also refuses the cereal. Hence, his breakfast is six pink, one blue and four yellow goblins.

<u>Lunch</u>: At school. Choice of sausage, pizza, coleslaw, diced carrot, chips, mashed potato. Followed by cake and strawberry custard. Benjy chooses mashed potato, chips, strawberry custard.

<u>Tea</u>: Marvellous, nutritious home-cooking by his adored Only-Mother-in-the-World, ie: Humid sprouts with consistency of hankie-contents, chicken nuggets, yesterday's potatoes heated up in V. Expensive olive oil (to introduce fake Euro-gourmet flavour). Benjy chooses one chicken nugget. Mother forgets to buy yoghurt for pudding so Benjy fills up on three packets of crisps, two choc rolls and nine biscuits in shape of dinosaurs.

He would probably do better on an unrestricted diet of fudge.

**Supermodels Arabella & Dianne reveal the secrets
of their Wonder Diet...**

Teenage Worriers before trying the Wonder Diet

Teenage Worriers after 3 months on the Wonder Diet

I wld personally like to open a Slow food chain,
especially for LURVErs, where the smells are so nice
but the service is so slow that they can get V. Excited
awaiting these sensory delights and entwine for the
several hours it took to get their meal which has been
baked at low temperatures in a simmering mass of
herbs and aphrodisiacs. Main items on menu at
L. Chubb's *Café Amoroso* wld be Ambrosia, elixir, and
fudge (limited menu, high profits heh heh). After some
years, regular customers wld be proven to have longer
life-spans, lower blood pressure, more Tranquil Souls
Etck, so it wld be V. Good for business in the end.

Not v.
sexy →

DRINK

Good consternoon
afterble. I'm not as think
as you drunk I am... hic

Teenage LURVers are often V. Tempted by booze to
reduce inhibitions Etck. A thimbleful of shandy and
I'm anybody's. Sadly, booze and lurve do not combine
however, as boyz' bods addle faster than their brains,
and willies often give up the struggle to stand upright
even quicker than their owners. I have always meant to
rewrite the story of Jekyll and Hyde as a Modern
Parable about the Evils of Alcohol, but I spect Kenneth
Branagh or someone will get in there first.

Beware any signs of evil temper, booze or drug
addiction in your beLURVed. If he turns from kindly
soul to Hitler and back again, be warned. As in Jekyll
and Hyde, these things start off small but you will soon
find that he is only the nice, kind bloke for about 3%

of the time. Anything he does now, he will do more and worse when he's 30. So get out while the going is good.

NB It is V. Diff, if plied with demon drink, to remember your partner's name, or even yr own. This can lead to Deep Regrets.

See telephone numbers at end of buke if you need more info.

DRUGS

At Sluggs, these are now as easy to get as sweeties. Luckily, there are enough kids who DON'T take them, so I don't feel ALONE.

Street drugs do not have aphrodisiac effect unless you fancy staring eyes, half a brain Etck. I have got even more V. Scared of drugs than when I wrote my last humble tome since I have now seen Ashley's old girlfriend going bonkers after taking something and having V.V. scary hallucinations. If you have fragile or Worried personality (ie: that is, like *moi*), it is best to steer clear of illegal substances especially since any dosh you pay out works its way up to people who really Don't Care. I know I sound like Granny Chubb, but if you have ever seen someone hallucinating, it wld stop you, too. I'll stick with fudge, thanks.

If you need more info on this subject – or any help – see telephone numbers at end of buke. Also, if you are worried about a FREND – you could save their LIFE.

CHAPTER FOUR
EEEEEEEEEZZE and FFFFFFFF

How strange is the Dark Hand of fate. I have just finished
the Deeeze in my humble alphabet . . . D oh, D. D is for
Desolation, doom, despond, dashed dreams, darkest despair,
dolour, dankness, and Banana itself. Also the Devil (who,
incidentally a V. Worrying number of the world's citizens
still say they believe in. So much for civilization, the Age of
Enlightenment, Etck). It is also for Daniel, who I will never
see again (at least not this week).

A Crisis has struck.

My only mother, who I always trusted (ah, sweet innocence
of childhood lost never to return) has READ this book. (Cups
hand to ear to catch sounds of wailing, renting of garments
Etck from Betrayed Teenage Worriers.)

However, dear Cheated Readers, although I am V.V.V.
angry at this Act of Betrayal and Unspeakable Intrusion into
my Privacy, she has also shamed me into seeing that I am a
V.V. Bad Person who is not fit to breathe (even in London,
where you're lucky to survive the pollution past 40, even with
your own personal ventilator and lifetime BUPA
membership).

For fairness' sake, and so you understand why I haven't
left home in high dudgeon Etck, I'll give HER side of the
story.

Having been forced by circs to attempt to gain access to the

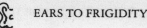

*Tyrannosaurus Kiss-Goodbye-To-Your-Cash money-box, I
found that all attempts failed, including hurling the
aforementioned monster at the wall, which only made it emit
a sound like a blender with a chicken inside it. Villainously,
I convinced Benjy it would be V.V. Interesting though noisy to
find out what it was like inside, and he dressed favourite
large teddy in his outdoor coat and woolly hat to watch at
close range while he withdrew to discreet distance, with
Horace in his cage for company. I put the Demon Dosh
Devourer on the floor and started on it with my adored
father's electric drill.*

*I thought I could see a place that looked as if it held the
whole thing together, but it was hard to keep the drill pointed
at it. Which is why, of course, it soon skidded off the grinning
Dinoprat and started eating the floorboards like the
Tasmanian Devil, instantly severing the central heating pipe
with a loud bang, sprays of steaming water, screams of Benjy
whose worst fears about floors are confirmed, crash of Horace's
cage as it overturns on to floor and door flies open and
hysterical gerbil exits left, wails and curses of L. Chubb
Etck, flailing around in sudden flood. Benjy ran downstairs
as fast as little legs would carry him after Horace, and out
into the street, closely pursued by moi fearing that Banana of
Ickle Brother under passing truck may be added to other
crimes.*

*Only mother charges in to find what she thinks is Benjy
lying drowning. She drags sodden figure of youngest offspring
out of torrent only to find he is a Teddy in a coat. I return to
Scene of Crime with Benjy happily clutching recaptured and
depressed-looking Horace, to find my Only Mother, damp and*

dishevelled, brandishing the scattered pages of my Great Work, which had been cast to the elements by her fierce making of my bed. Behind this horrible scene I glimpse Only

Jurassic Spark: Moi versus Doshiverous Rex

Father railing at misuse of his beloved drill, though looking secretly pleased at role of Man of House *going off to look for fuse boxes, stopcocks Etck.*

Resulting dialogue with Only Mother *includes the following:*

Part One *(on general theme of Mess, Mayhem Etck)*
    1) *'Are you mad?'*
    2) *'Are you trying to kill us all?'*
    3) *'Do you realize you could have gone through mains cable, electrocuted yourself and Benjy and burned us all in our beds?'* (*she was only* making *the bed, not in bed, but it didn't seem the moment to point this out) and,*

Part Two *(on theme of contents of Great Work, waved contemptuously under conspicuous nose of L. Chubb)*
    1) *'How* COULD *you be so underhand as to plan to steal your friend's boyfriend?'*
    2) *'Don't you realize what a sad life Aggy has had?'* *(There followed a lot of cringey details about her Wicked White mother running off with the postman and Aggy having to help her poor Black, sharing, caring Dad with her ten zillion siblings, and her eye problems, and being horizontally challenged — my mother has got V. Politically Correct since working at the Kiddies' Library, and doesn't just say 'Fat' any more.)*
    3) *'And as for* robbing your own grandmother, *frankly I'm lost for words.'*

This didn't stop her from thinking of a lot more words, each

*one piercing a deeper hole in my already anguished psyche. She
even accused me (moi!) of racism! Just 'cos I made the odd
throwaway jest about Spiggy's homeland being overrun with
upside-down convicts! Whoever said words can't hurt you
needs a brain transplant. When she got to the bit about how I
could have drowned an ailing Rover in her basket as well, I
couldn't take any more. I dissolved in a flood of self-
recrimination and cried more tears than Alice down the rabbit
hole. I blame Spiggy for leading me Astray. Whatever my
Only Mother says, Australians are all descended from
prisoners anyway and look what they did to the indignant
people of their own Nation. (I have a feeling it's meant to be
'indigenous' but I'd have been more likely to be indignant if I
was them.)*

*I shall forget our Plan, refuse to speak to Spiggy, put
everything I own into Opening New Horizons for Granny
Chubb, and while on the subject save up for some Contact
Lenses for Aggy too, so she will look all right on her wedding
to the Most Wonderful Boy In The Universe, argh, yeeech,
guilt, glow of self-sacrifice Etck.*

*But how will I ever earn enough to see my mother through
the menopause? To rescue my father from the nervous
breakdown he is obviously having (otherwise why would he be
saying we don't need a phone, or electricity, or any of the
other things he can't pay for)? Or to pay for a child
psychiatrist for Benjy, who has already been having dreams
that he is Aladdin hurtling through space on a magic lino,
even before I made the bedroom floor turn into Mount
Vesuvius?*

*I must work night and day on my alphabet, it is my only
hope.*

EEEEEEEEEES

Eı**ARS**

The Ears (espesh the LOBES) are a major erogenous zone, which means if they are nibbled or stroked by the right person, you can feel the effect all over yr Bod. V. Large flappy ones like mine do not apparently respond more erogenously than Hazel's V. delicate shell-like ones, so sadly there is no compensation, as Dumbo's mother knew.

NB. V. Imp to check yr hearing regularly so you can catch those whispered sweet nothings. Also, V. Embarrassing if you hear them wrong as happened to me on one occasion when I thought this V. Handsome boy was whispering:

'Letty, oh! Letty, oh!'

when in fact his feverish cry was:

'Let me go! Let me go!'

Well, it was a V. Noisy party and how was I to know he was gay?

EJACULATION

This is when the boy reaches a sexual climax, when sperm go charging up the willy and rushing out the

end, cheering and wagging their tails, only to thump
into a condom (we hope) and then swim about for a bit,
V. Depressed like goldfish in a milkbottle, before
finally snuffing it. Do not feel sorry for the luckless
sperms though, because if they all got their own way
we wld all be standing shoulder to shoulder on The
Planet and fighting for a grain of rice, wiping out vast
hordes in Battles For Survival Etck, even more than we
are now.

ELOPEMENT

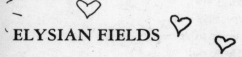

Q: If two ants ran off to marry, would they be an Antelope?

Running away to get married without parents'
permishun. Since my adored father thinks the
Institution of Marriage is all bourgwois crepe anyway,
it will be an act of rebellion if I walk up aisle in big
white dress.

ELYSIAN FIELDS

Glorious place where the Greeks believed you could go
if you were V. Good. Always sunny, with nothing but
Good Behaviour, magical food, sublime music Etck. I
intend, when rich, to name one of my estates Elysium.
The fields that surround it will then be Elysian fields in
which Daniel and I will gambol, strumming our lyres,
Etck.

EMBARRASSMENT

Teenagers in LURVE cannot navigate the slopes and ravines of Passion's Mountain without pitfalls, and Embarrassment is a constant companion on this Vital Journey. Blushes can be V. fetching, if only you cld control them for the right moments, but shades of the lobster sadly usually visit your cheeks just as you are trying to look Pale and Interesting.

Mixing up letters can be very embarassing, e.g. sending steamy missive above to aunty who sent you a beige cardy for Christmas

Here is an Eg: You are keen to impress your beLURVed's parents but Embarrassing Stuff leaps Cackling and Gibbering from the hardworking Embarrassment Dept deep inside the Self-Destruct Zone in yr Head, viz:

'Oh I know, Mrs Coy, those little secrets between a mother and her son! Well, I've got a mole in almost exactly the same place, believe it or not . . .'

Then there's all the usual terrible stuff like treading dog-poo all over their brand new beige carpets, throwing up into their Scandinavian-style sink after one glass of birthday champagne, leaving items of underwear in their Adored Son's bedroom Etck.

ENGAGEMENTS: see WEDDINGS

ERECTION ← No drawing. I refuse to be CENSORED again.

As readers of my best-selling blah blah I WAS A TEENAGE WORRIER (buy now while socks last Etck) will know, an erection is what happens to a Boy'z willy when it receives message from the Optic Bits re sighting of L. Chubb's sinuous, silky, sumptuous Etck form. Blood thunders furiously through tiny vessels of said member, and organ stands to attention to take its place in history of human race, possibly rendering Higher Being attached by nervous system, bloodvessels Etck to rampant organ liable to paternity suits.

Paternity suits are not shortsleeved Fair Isle jumpers and baggy beige corduroys as worn by Caring Fathers in Natural Childbirth videos, but Full Weight Of The Law as hurled by bizarre toffs in half-specs and wigs rightly demanding appropriate Dosh for Surprised Single Mum to cope with New Life after eruption of rampant organ into enthusiastic Female Bits Etck.

Boyz Worry a lot about whether their willies will get hard, or stay hard at the right time and whether they will get hard or stay hard at the wrong time. According to Ashley, these thoughts occupy huge vistas of Boyz' brains which explains a lot to yr av female Teen Worrier. Of course, Boyz think that this is just Their Problem, that none of their mates have the same fears Etck, and that if they do not perform in this respect Gurlz will giggle about them in loos, take out full-page ads in newspapers that their willies are invisible to all but David Attenborough-type stick insect documentaries, compare them to former LURVErs whose willies required the bedroom wall to be knocked down before they could get in the room Etck. However, if Boyz' willies do not work properly, the prob is usually V. Temporary, and if it isn't, V. Sympathetic expert help can be obtained (See phone nos at end of buke).

EROTICA

Anything that turns you on. As you grow to Teenage Worrier status, you begin to realize there are a V. Large number of Strange Things people find erotic, some of which I cannot go into in a Family Book such as this or you will be raided by Dirty Books Squad Etck and this noble tome never seen again except as Exhibit A in High Court and at Dirty Books Squad Christmas Party. People find all kinds of things give them shivers, hot flushes Etck. In one V. Steamy video I saw round at Hazel's house when her parents were out, Mickey Rourke liked melting ice on to Kim Basinger's disrobed Bod – I have tried this on *moi* but laughed so much Benjy came in and tipped the whole jug of ice

Q: Do cats need Erotica?

over my head, from which he narrowly escaped with his
Life, but still brought the subject up at breakfast next
day. Ickle brothers do not walk into Lives of Mickey
Rourke, Kim Basinger Etck; I wonder why. Then
there's all kinds of V. Weird stuff to do with underwear,
rubber, spanking Etck which I will not go into here
because of a) Dirty Books Squad, pillorying of L.
Chubb in Parliament, *D. Telegraph* Etck and b) because
I think most Teenage Worriers, however Worried they
are about their Desirability Etck, do not yet need all

this stuff to get Excited, Ardent, Steamy Etck because
they are like it most of the time at this stage of Life
anyway. It is a bit of a Shame that maybe we will grow
up to find LURVE with that Special Person a bit
Boring and need to go in for all this V. Corny Posing
around, imagining we are really with a fifteen-stone gas
fitter from Basildon in a welding helmet, being
punished by Teacher Etck. But for fresh Teen Worriers,
who are not jaded in the ways of Lurve, almost
anything DOES turn us on. Viz: Glimpse of
beLURVEd's trainers; sound of beLURVEd chewing
gum; merest touch of beLURVEd's sweatshirt, turn of
their head, curve of their lashes (no, you pervert, I
mean eyelashes) Etck Etck. Who needs a fetish when
you're a Teenager-in-LURVE?

ETIQUETTE

This means how to behave, and used to be V. Imp.
There were trillions of rules about how to say hello to
different types of folk, thousands of LURVE rules for
Dating, proposals, chaperones Etck which the Yoof
then took V. Little notice of, as always.

Still, a return to Etiquette might be a V. Good
Thing. Children being Seen But Not Heard, wld be
great in the case of Benjy, though at the times when he
is wearing his food, seeing him isn't so hot either.

Return of Etiquette might be good thing in some cases...

EYES

Windows to soul and therefore V. Good Guide in my humble opinion, as to how someone is feeling about you. One thing LURVErs shld definitely know: the pupil enlarges when looking at something (or someone – swooon) it likes, and shrinks when observing a nauseating object. However, do not be too disturbed if your beLURVEd's pupil disappears when you gaze into his peepers, as it cld just be that His Parents suddenly switched on the 4 Mill. Watt Alcatraz-style Anti-Nooky searchlight and his pupils shrank in self-protection. This must be one of the reasons most LURVERS favour candlelight. It gives them a headstart in the dilated pupil stakes as well as romantic glow, Etck.

I long for azure eyes the colour of Spring skies Etck (like DH's) or verdant eyes brighter than brussel sprouts and slimmer than cats' eyes (like Hazel's), or smouldering eyes the colour of melting chocolate (like that teacher I had a crush on, or even Aggy, spit, gnash) but mine cld best be described as slate. Or sludge.

FFFFFFFFFFFFFFFFFFFFFFFFFF

FALLOPIAN TUBES

If you want lotsa details about reproduction, you're in the wrong book. Still, a book about LURVE shld mention I feel, 'the Oviduct in female mammals' ie: the little tubes in Gurlz that take the egg from the ovary and down which we all must travel to get to the womb. The beginning of Life's mysterious journey . . .

FAMILY

LURVE starts here. In fact, many middle-aged worriers spend small fortunes on therapy just to be told that the reason they can't hang on to a job, relationship, money Etck and the fact that even their pet gerbils put in for a

transfer is all because they were not sufficiently LURVEd as ickle babas. Clearly, this is V. Unfair on their poor old Mums, Dads Etck who probably did their best, but I must admit some Bad Starts must take a lot of recovering from.

On adverts for washing powder, vacuum cleaners, DIY Etck, and in Hollywood PG movies, they have people playing the parts of Families who they obviously

Families: Fiction...

get from Virtual Reality machines, genetic-engineering Family Farms, Other Planets Etck. They all have V. White teeth, wear big jumpers and talk in that V. Bright, Clear, Cheery way people address Mad Folk or V. Small Children. They keep this up even while in the middle of Completely Suicidal things like washing up, ironing Etck. Nobody believes they exist, but since they seem to live in a World without Worries, Rows, Accidents, Disasters, Poverty Etck, people buy the stuff because they hope they might start feeling a bit like this as soon as they open the packet.

Despite knowing the ads are all Rubbidge, I do sometimes dream of a kind, handsome Dad who brings

... and Fact

home the bacon yet still has time to play football, Scrabble Etck, and serene mother looking like Nanette Newman and overflowing with LURVE, malted milk drinks Etck. If you've got just one parent who is a little like either of these, then you are better off than 99% of World Population and shouldn't whinge . . . (easier said than done, moan, gnash, hair shirt, guilt). And, sadly, some families are a lot more unlike the Perfect fantasy than mine. If yours are cruel, ring Childline. See phone numbers at back of buke.

FANCYING *Phew squirm*

First stage, as all Teenage Worriers know, of LURVE. If you do not fancy someone, there is no point in pursuing LURVE. It will never feel right, and never come (as t'were).

FASHION

What to wear has been constant worry for Teenagers in LURVE but in recent years it has luckily been solved by L. Chubb's Uniform.

This can be worn on all occasions and will suit most shapes and sizes.

Top: V.V. Big sweatshirt with V.V. long arms (necessary in case of *moi*). Light grey is favoured colour of mid-nineties Kool yoof, but I am promoting pink in

next season's catalogue. Buy six of these and you only have to wash them about twice a year.

Bottom: V.V. Baggy jogging pants (black).

Feet: Four pairs socks (three in summer) and DMs (black).

Variations: One black top for nightclubs (I will have to keep this in special lead-lined, high-security Fort Knox-type wardrobe to keep out damp, moths, Benjy Etck until the day about five million years from now when my Adored Parents finally let me go to one. But it may be out of Fashion then, boo hoo, aargh, curses Etck. Nobody else allowed to wear one until L. Chubb's Liberation Night). Plus L. Chubb's range of T-Shirts (see pics) which will be in shops soon as long as I can sign up Vivienne Westwood to manufacture them. Please write to V.W. asking where they are.

Accessories: One individual item that is your trademark. In my case it's a waistcoat and sometimes a top with hearts on. These may not seem Kool to you, but I am confident that they suit *moi* (argh, worry, do I really look that silly, why didn't you tell me when I did the first book, argh blush, it's too late to change the cover of this one, bury head in hole, rail at cruel world Etck).

NB Don't try to jazz up the outfit with a little scarf or belt as advised by *Smirk* Etck. Simplicity is the key to Knock-Em-Dead Style. Wish I could learn this rule myself as am prone to draping spindly frame in multicoloured layers of stuff (partly to add bulk, partly to hide basic form) and end up looking like Barber's Pole.

That's enough about fashion. You can read zillions of daft articles about it every week in about 2,000 publications, and all you do is spend every tinkle of dosh you've been able to extract from Cruel and Uncaring World, and end up with drawers full of belts, earrings, velcro snap mini skirts, tie-dye bell bottoms Etck Etck that you wouldn't be seen dead in two minutes after you bought them.

PS: Also V. Worried about much-heralded return of Glamour (ie: fishnet tights, wonder-bras, cleavage, sequins Etck which are not my style at all but seem sadly V. Popular with Boyz). Is my brief skylight of opportunity as a SuperWaif to be Over before it has Begun??

V. Worried about
return to Glamour...

Fishnets
My own
spindly shanks
wld. protrude
through holes...

Stillettos
Make moi look
like Minnie
Mouse.
Thought:
could use
Fabu-bra as Ears.

FIANCE

Him to whom you are engaged to be married. Add an
'e' and it becomes her to whom you are engaged to be
married. I don't much fancy the idea of getting
engaged *moi*self, it wld be sad if you just turned out to
be a passing fiancee (ha ha, yeech, old jokes always best
Etck).

FLATTERY

Flattery will get you everywhere, is the motto of L. Chubb. Anyway, it has to be laid on with a trowel before anyone dislikes it, because however modest you may be, you tend to believe nice things said to you. Frinstance I find Daniel's mention of my 'nervous fawnlike grace' keeps recurring in my innermost thoughts and much improving my er, self image, though sometimes I think he might have meant I just look Worried and have V. Thin legs. Also, if you gaze into someone's eyes and tell them how clever they are, you will notice them blush and preen. If you want them to like you, dear reader, a little flattery goes a V. Long way . . . and what may appear nauseatingly obsequious to anyone in their right mind, will seem like the pinnacle of insight to the recipient of the compliment. But don't lay it on TOO thick. A smattering of compliments to begin with, and an air of detachment, should be enough to arouse maximum interest. Eg: 'I've heard you're a genius at chess. I only wish I was good enough to share it with you' (this should get you a chess lesson V. Fast).

Or: 'Is it true that at your last school all the girls were mad about you? You're not really my type, but I can certainly see why.'

Mark Twain said he could live for two months on a good compliment, and certainly I've found the recollection of the few glorious things that Daniel said

to me most nourishing in the Dark Night of my Soul. He has frinstance said such things as: 'I LURVE the way yr nose wrinkles when you giggle' and 'you look like a Supermodel from the back'. I realize these things are not quite the same as 'when I look at you I want us to be together until Hell freezes over' or even 'you make me want to tear all my clothes off and make LURVE for a week without stopping' but in a drought, you have to be glad of whatever droplets of brackish water you can get, that's Wot I Say.

111

FLIRTING

Flirting is like being tickled when you were a baby . . .
it's a game where you both know the rules, and the
only point of it is to give you that warm shiver up and
down yr spine. Flirting is often done without words at
all and involves Soulful, Questioning or Downright
Suggestive little twitches and twirls of all those tiny
little eye muscles that make us look completely
different from one second to the next, or brief, fluttery
little touches on the arm, leaning against you a little
too long while looking at a magazine Etck. Flirting is
One Of The Great Delights Of The World when
coming from someone you like the look of, and V.
Unwelcome or just Plain Boring from someone you
don't. Under new PC rules written by Bossy Worried
People in the States, they are trying to make even V.
Mild forms of Flirting into Harassment, throwing
people out of jobs for brushing against yr sleeve Etck.
Real Harassment though, which can include somebody
flirting V. Heavily with you when you've made it V.
Clear you don't want them to, shld not be tolerated. If
somebody goes on doing it, complain to a Teacher or yr
Parents.

See also 'NO'.

FLOWERS

The language of LURVE is spoken by flowers and there

are V. Good books on their langwidge if you want to be
subtle. But why spend a fortune on red roses that wilt
in minutes when you could pick a humble spray of
forget-me-nots and say the same thing for a quarter the
price? Not that money should be any object in LURVE
(if I had any my true LURVE wld have to get the staff
of Kew Gdns in to water the bouquets). L. Chubb says:
Give the Boy of your Dreamz Flowers. Unusual.
Imaginative. And a V. Big Guilt trip too as he will
think: 'But I have never given her flowers. Surely I
don't deserve this? She must think me V. Special' at
which point he will ponder, preen and prob run a mile.
In which case console yourself that he was not Boy For
You. His other response will be to get you a bigger
bunch and you will know you are In With A Chance.

LURVERS' TIP: Grow an ickle flower from seed. If the
person you are in LURVE with when it blooms is the
same person you were in LURVE with when you
planted it (V. Unlikely but Hope springs Eternal), then
pick it and give it to them.

FOREPLAY: see SEX

FRIENDS

'A Friend in need is a friend indeed.' I have often
wondered whether this means that a friend who needs

YOU is a true friend, or that a true friend is someone
who is kind when YOU need them?

I think it is the latter, but I must say, until V.
Recently I have always been the listening shoulder, as
t'were Etck, and after all I did for Aggy I must admit
to more than a little sense of BETRAYAL. However,
Spiggy, despite being Australian and in love with a
Malteser, has been a V. Good Friend-in-Need to me.
And Hazel was V. Kind to me after Daniel left, so I am
V. Lucky really and I know there are plenty of Teenage
Worriers who have no friend in all the world (sob) and

no-one to turn to, so who am I to complain about the dastardly treachery of Aggy? Grind, gnash, sweet revenge . . .

I shall rise above it only to say I wld go to the Ends of the Earth for my True Frendz and that LURVErs may come and go but friendship is a constant beacon to guide you through life's perilous swamp and that if you have found a True Frend, do not let her go (or Betray her by Stealing her Man). We Gurlz must stick together as boyz are V. Fickle.

FRIGIDITY

If you hear a boy say a Gurl is frigid, it means she told him she wouldn't Do It with him, because if she really meant she was shy or uncertain about SEX (as 99.9% of Teenage Worriers are at some time or another) and he LURVEd her anyway, he wouldn't tell people.

Many Teenage Worriers wonder if they are Frigid and try to prove they aren't by doing lots of stuff they don't really enjoy, which gives them even more reason to believe they're Frigid. Dear reader, if you have never felt any Longings, it is V. Unlikely you are frigid. It is almost certain that you have just not found the person who Turns You On. This person may not be the one you expect (viz Hazel who did it with zillions of Boyz before falling in LURVE with a Gurl) but rest assured you will Know When You Meet Them. Or, perhaps, Touch them. Or, indeed, get touched by them (cold shower, bucket of water over steaming Bod Etck).

NB Never let anyone make you do something you don't like because they are saying you're Frigid; it's a Big Lie to cover their own Fears, Worries Etck.

CHAPTER FIVE
GEEEEEEEZE and HHHHHH

Please don't be shocked, but, ahem, I have changed my mind.

Look, I didn't speak to Spiggy for nearly two whole days, I would have put the phone down on her if it had been working. But she was so upset I had to explain.

Well, she made me see it differently.

After all, I had been going out with Daniel before Aggy stole him off me. Also, our plan wasn't to lure him back by false pretences, but merely, um, to confront him with a choice between his Innermost Desires and his Duties as a Great Human Being to a visually challenged person with a Morally Challenged mum. 'All's fair', concluded Spiggy with startling originality, 'in Lurve and War.'

I did have a twingette of doubt. I knew Aggy had yearned for Daniel even before I'd met him and that she was after all flying off to visit her Only-Mother-in-the-World who she hadn't seen for a year and who she was hoping to persuade to return to the nest in order to keep her Only-Father-in-the-World from the clutches of Fancy Women, and her adored but loony siblings from the clutches of the local constabulary Etck. But I brushed these thoughts aside as my bazoom swelled — well, twitched anyway — at the thought of Daniel's embrace. Shiver, melt Etck (you don't know what it feels like to boil and freeze simultaneously, dear reader, until you have truly LURVED).

Anyway, I am still going to do loads of Good Works to raise money for G. Chubb, and have worked out special cut-rate military operation (in line with impending New World Order cheapo Brit defence policy of reducing cost of army to one man and V. Loud tape recording of Dam Busters raid). Ergo, reducing DHAM transport charges by cycling four tube stations down the line to get into cheaper zone, borrowing bandages from Spiggy's Flying Doc father's surgery, make-up from Benjy's face paints, and fake blood (to dab on my bandages in the Airport Reunion saga, swoooon) from his Instant-Ghoul-Give-Your-Parents-A-Coronary kit. To make it up to him for everything, I have babysat Benjy four nights this week, and it means my adored parents can go out and bond too (which they badly need) though it took some persuading to convince them that I wasn't going to try Semtex to blow the jeering head off the Tyrannosaurus Money-Muncher while they were out.

So my conscience is assuaged. Only two days to go till Friday. I have told my mother I will be staying that night at Hazel's. She is V. Chuffed as she always is when I see Hazel, because she thinks Hazel has posh frendz and a vast Network of people with V. Loud Voices whose daddies own banks, boats, armies of mumbling servants Etck. This is an Eg of her political correctness blurring somewhat when it comes to seeing her ickle chickadees Getting On, whatever that is.

Anyway, just for once, I am V. Glad the phone is on the blink as my Only Mother will not be able to check my story.

Rover seems to have caught my mood and has taken a little minced fish. I am the only one who ever cooks for her; all my mother gives her are cheapo tins, although Granny Chubb says they are quite tasty if you stir in a dash of Tabasco and a stock cube. In a burst of goodwill I played Batman for ten whole minutes with Benjy, but sadly it came home to roost as he dreamt Rover had turned into Catwoman and was eating Horace out of a tin.

Spiggy has not heard from her Malteser for ten days, so we wallow abjectly together. I tell her it is bound to be the post, as since Aggy's mother deserted with the postman I have V. grate suspicions of said officials. Anyway, how long can star-crossed lurve last, when a world separates Spiggy from her beLURVed? Never mind . . . soon Daniel will take me away from all this. I wish I'd never burnt his letters . . . all I have to put under my pillow is a piece of gum personally chewed by him that I found stuck to my foot when we had our one unforgettable soirée by the river. I have glued it to a heart-shaped piece of pink card but it still doesn't look V. Romantic and I fear I may have trodden on something else as well as the gum.

GAMES

When you played Doctors and Nurses, Cars and Garages, Boats and Harbours and (whoops, yes, I admit it) Hide the Sausage in Primary School, you were preparing for Life's great experience of LURVE. This is why Parents have often pretended these things don't go on, because they like to think of childhood as a Time of Innocence, when children's idea of fun is only Batman,

Polly Pockets Etck. Imagine what the ads would look like if children's grosser interests were catered for! 'See Cutesy Angie's nipples pop up when she kisses Hunky Harry!' 'Happy hours of fun with All-Action SUPALURVER with working trouser-bulge!'

As far as *moi* is concerned, I only wish I was as uninhibited now as I was then in my joyous infancy when Boyz and Gurlz showed each other their bits with cheerful abandon. Posh schools say Games are a V. Good preparation for Life's Battles, Life Isn't Fair, Sink or Swim, Survival of Fittest Etck, but I think they

I long to return to joyous infancy when Boyz and Gurlz showed each other their bits with cheerful abandon

mean the kind where you hurl yourself into fray, and most vicious player emerges victorious. This may all be true in our sad, competitive, thrusting, everyone-for-themselves-No-Such-Thing-As-Society world, but I dream of a future where Teenage Worriers cld play Doctors and Nurses with their Sex Tutors and learn to be less Loony SEXual beings than we are now. After all, some societies go on about the Arts of LURVE which strikes me as a V. Good Thang.

Other LURVE games are closely related to Flirting Etck. See FLIRTING.

GAY

Someone once said that if Michelangelo had been
straight, the Sistine chapel wld have been wallpapered,
and I can't help noticing that a lot of V. Artistick,
clever people of both sexes who have achieved the
equivalent of Not Wallpapering The Sistine Chapel
have been Gay.

I am convinced that I am Heterosexual at the
moment, as I am sure I would fancy Hazel otherwise.
In fact, Hazel's recent about-turn has made me ponder
this subject more deeply, as what has made me V. Sad
about it is she doesn't want her family (or her friends at
the posh Girls Academy) to know. This means she lives
a life of Subterfuge and Anguish and whereas if she had
gone on being heterosexual she might have had to keep
the details of Wild Nooky with a Boy from her parents,
at least she wld be able to Hold Hands in Public.
Anyone who thinks times have changed and that it's
easy to be Lesbian these days, should look at Hazel and
Think again.

Join L. Chubb's campaign for Safe Sexual Freedom!
Actually, Lesbianism is the best way to avoid both
AIDS and unwanted pregnancies, though I am not of
course saying it shld be Compulsory. Maybe if Having
Babies gets to be just a matter of mailing a couple of
test-tubes to a laboratory, allow 28 days for delivery of
brand-new fully working baba, thaw at room
temperature for 4 hrs and then tickle under chin,
fizzical LURVE will get to be much freer. I realize this

is a V. Controversial Matter, esp with Religious Folk, of which I am sometimes one, but it is an Interesting Discussion Point if you have a few years free.

Anyway, It is V. Upsetting for Teenage Worriers to have to conceal their sexual preferences (as if there wasn't enough to dog their lives, troubles of world on shoulders, no futures, 'what's a job, Dad?' Etck).

Boyz who are Gay have always been given V. Hard time by oicks Etck, who think if they shout 'Poof' and 'Fairy' everyone will think they are V. Butch. Or 'Men's Men'.

End tyranny, says Fearless El Chubb. So that all LURVErs, old ones (like Granny and Grandpa Chubb, sob, wish he was still with us), young ones, Boyz with Boyz, Gurlz with Gurlz and all combinations could gambol in Elysian fields in (or out of) silken robes for Eternity without having teachers, social workers Etck telling them how big their Problem is. Naturally, I do mean LURVErs should be Consenting Adults.

If you think you are Gay and you are not lucky enough to have a V. Good Frend who is also Gay, it is V. Imp to find Frendz who know what they are on about. See list of Useful phone numbers in back of this humble tome.

End this tyranny, says El Chubb, so that all
LURVERS can gamble, I mean gambol, in Elysian
Fields for Eternity

GOD

God is LURVE, they say. He watcheth every sparrow
fall. He Cares. Well. He'd better, 'cos I often think
nobody else does, sigh, moan, self-pity Etck. Sometimes
I wail, 'Help! Help me get Daniel back! What is the
Meaning of Life Etck if such things can happen?' And I
think to myself, 'No, I won't pray REALLY hard yet, in
case things get worse and I've wasted all my prayers
already so God just thinks, 'Oh no, not *her* again'.'

But although I still have a V. Innocent, Narnia-type
Faith in an all-LURVing Being, I have noticed that lots
of people start to get cynical at about my age. I don't
know why, I should have thought Cyberspace and
Virtual Reality and Artificial Intelligence Etck would
have made people more religious, not less. After all, if
it *is* possible for puny old Humans to build something
that knows everything and can recall it in an instant,
why shouldn't Some*one* have already evolved out there
in the Universe and be able to do all that and more,
with the power of LURVE to boot? See also
RELIGION.

GOING OUT

I have written at length in my previous tome about
how to get a Date Etck, but have since been pondering
on phrase: Going Out. Teen Worriers in my part of
town are all doing their utmost to STAY IN with the

person they're 'GOING OUT' with, so they can get their mitts on their naughty bits. Parents are sublimely unaware of how frequently the V. responsible Teenage babysitter they have hired is just using their gaff to invite their BELURVed round for illicit fondling, canoodling Etck.

However, Teen Worriers are V. Keen to get 'going out' type dates also, as it wld not be perlite to use first date for nooky on borrowed sofa (at least not till you've been out somewhere first).

GORGON

Female monster from Greek Mythology with snakes for hair and eyes that turned people to stone.

Men like to think that women are V. Powerful and can have this effect on them though as far as I know there has been no example of it in Real Life except Psychologically. (Lots in stories, however, viz: Delilah taking away Samson's power just by giving him a haircut, Lady Macbeth urging The Old Man to do the Dirty Work, Etck.)

This confirms the L. Chubb theory (V. Original and unthought of by anyone else, *naturellement*) that men are V.V. Scared of Women and think if they give us Power Over Our lives then their Willies won't work Etck.

Since it is V.V. Imp for women that men's willies DO continue to work – partly 'cos women are quite Kindly Souls and partly 'cos of Future of Human

Species, and partly 'cos Doing It is Fun (so I hear, weep, moan, gnash), us Gurlz bend over backwards to please men, assure them we are not gorgons Etck and therefore do not want to become Managing Directors, World leaders Etck but wld rather stay home minding our business and the kids so they mustn't be frightened.

So, the imbalance of Power between the sexes continues for another ten generations. And all because of a Gorgon.

GROUPIE

Many Teenage Worriers hover outside dressing rooms, hotels Etck in a vain hope of catching a fleeting glimpse of The Hero.

However, trying to catch a fleeting or even prolonged glimpse of parts of The Hero that do not normally appear in Family Newspapers Etck, ie: viz, attempting to Do It with said Person is V. Dangerous and L. Chubb advises you not to, and not just out of Sour Grapes, Envy Etck Etck either. Celebs with V. Big Egos and (possibly) Other Bits to match may sound V. Flattering about you while you are in the Romantic, True LURVE circs of trying to locate yr zip, or his, for the three-and-a-half minutes he's granting you in his dressing room, but they Never Mean It and if you try to phone them afterwards it's as if they were never there.

Luckily, most of you sophisticated Teenage Worriers will be past the drivelling phase of Groupiedom, but for those of you who are not, remember it is best to keep Stars where they should be, viz looking byootyful at a safe distance, for if you get too close they may burn you to a crisp. Try instead, dear reader, to see yr Frendz and Family for the Stars they are (yaaah, boo, soppy, gerroff Etck) and LURVE them for themselves.

HHHHHHHHHHHHHHHHHH

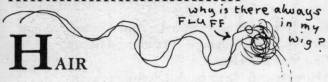

why is there always FLUFF in my wig?

Hair

In its natural state, my hair makes me look like an Afghan Hound with the wind behind it. Trouble is, whenever I try to do anything different with it, I end up looking like someone else, and it's never somebody I want to look like.

When you swan into swanky hair salons they show you loads of pics of V. Byootiful women with V. Byootiful Hair. What they are trying to get you to believe all seems backwards to me. What I wld like to do wld be to choose a face from the magazines and keep my own hair, which wld look fine with a different face hanging under it.

Instead, I am forced into a macabre green overall (green is NOT my Lucky Colour), examined by someone who looks as if she wishes hairdressers were allowed surgeons' masks, who exclaims: 'Who cut this last?' It's not always easy to see exactly what she's driving at, but all the alternatives are Bad News. Either it means the last person deserves danger money for trying, or Capital Punishment for ruining yr life for ever.

Stage Two involves being hurled backwards into a basin and pummelled with unguents. Does this hurt everyone? Or is it just 'cos I am V. Bony?

The Strange Power of the Salon has me in thrall...

Then they comb it, pretending to put foot in yr back to get necessary leverage Etck, breaking combs, dislocating wrists Etck. At this stage I realize I have Changed my Mind and want to keep it Long. But by now, the Strange Power of the Salon, with its stainless steel uplighting and Dracula-Wing Mirrors, has me in Thrall, and anyway they're not letting me out without the chance for Vengeance. I am Speechless. I watch, distraught, as my lifesavings and my life's wig are cut down in their prime. The floor is carpeted with wig clippings, appallingly revealing Head as miniscule shining Sphere balancing precariously on stalk like lolly on stick. Woe, gnash Etck.

Well, that's how my only visit to the hairdressers seems to me now. Suddenly my only mother's quick trim of my locks every three months seems The Stuff of Dreams by comparison, even though I always accused her of Wrecking my Life each time she did it.

It will be a while before I can afford to get a proper haircut again. When I do, I'll borrow the local Rottweiler (from the bloke with tattoos who takes his jogging past our house and keeps telling it to 'effing SHUT IT!') and tie it up outside the shop, just to let them know what might happen if they don't listen to what I want. Meanwhile, I shall dream of perms (even though the one Hazel once did on me made me look like Louis XIV), highlights, lowlights Etck Etck and everything but the bird's nest soup ingredients that really do cover my nut.

Why is it that Hazel's silky waterfall of a mane is

maintenance-free? That Aggy just lets hers frizz like a loo-brush and still gets my Man? That confident Spiggy just runs a comb through hers without needing to winch it with a Land Rover, and then looks OK with a hairslide of all things? Worry, worry, worry.

HAIR TIP: Teenage Worriers can lose confidence with wrong hairdo. Do not cut hair to please someone else.

Hair has been known to affect confidence of
Teenage Worriers

HAMMOCK

If I cld get Daniel beside me in a hammock, he'd never GET OUT. This is my ambition. It wld be slung twixt two palm trees on a silver beach. Swooooon.

NB Doing It in a hammock strikes me as a risky business, although the opportunity to discover *how* risky might be worth the danger element. Anyway, you are likely to go hurtling into the garden four doors down if you get too animated, or even into the Next Dimension, thus discovering time travel, which wld definitely be Worth It. NB 2 – must sell Back To The Future in Hammock idea to Hollywood ASAP.

HAPPINESS

What LURVE-is-all-about.

How do we find it? That is life's journey.

Why do we want it? 'Cos we're unhappy without it.

When do we want it? Now.

BUT (NB this is called 'a big but') it is worth pondering a Big Question and that is, how do we Measure Happiness? Frinstance, we know LURVE can make you V.V. Unhappy and that a mug of hot choccy has opposite effect, but what occupies a Teenage Worrier's seedy brain the most? LURVE? or Hot Choc?

Most people wld prob say, if there was a *Happiness Survey*, that the most important things to them wld be: Being with someone they like; doing something they like; living somewhere they like. Which means: People, work, home. In the case of *moi*, that wld mean making films on horseback with Daniel Hope, outside our mountain retreat (within easy reach of waterfalls, beaches, superstores Etck). Swoon.

LURVE
Happiness rating:
Zero to Zillions
(usually zero, sob)

HOT CHOCCY
Happiness rating:
A reliable one
hundred.

Thinks: Does the above tell us something about the Nature of the universe? Worry, worry...

But I also think that unless you are capable of being pretty happy come what may, LURVE's pleasures will probably elude you, as moaning on does not attract either frendz or lurvers. I think now of Lisa, in my class at Sluggs, whose nickname of moaner Lisa has nothing to do with her enigmatic smirk, but a lot to do with her snivelling about tummy aches, boyz, horrid teachers, food, world Etck all the time.

All this leads *moi* to believe that 'Happiness comes from within'. This fabulous original thought from L. Chubb can be embroidered at little cost onto T-shirts, coasters Etck and bought at knock down prices from the publisher. Meanwhile, please campaign for a HAPPINESS SURVEY to be conducted world wide so we can discover if people living in one room in Novosibirsk are, surprisingly, happier queueing all day for half a slice of salami than people living on mountain retreats near superstores Etck. If we cld discover this, Nature of Universe and answer to life's probs wld be crystal clear. I have a sneaky feeling the answers wld reveal that to LURVE and be LURVED wld rate pretty high, but maybe solitude, or loadsa dosh really are the answer. Viz: if the National Lottery was for a year with the Person of Your Dreams, would there be as many takers?

HAREM

A whole bunch of wives as enjoyed by rich sheiks Etck.

I wld be V. Pleased with an array of husbands with DH as chief, but wld not like to queue up for a Sheik, Rattle & Roll Etck.

HEART

The Heart is meant to be where it all happens — LURVE that is. Personally I have never thought the kind of Heart you see with Cupid's arrow sticking through it bears much resemblance to the horrible, pink, bulgy, yeechy thing with tubes sprouting out of it they show in the medical books Benjy's always looking at. (He mostly looks at other Bits of the Bod, and rolls on the floor cackling at how daft the Human Person he's going to grow up into really is.)

Would you put a real heart on your Valentine Card?

But of course, the Heart is the giveaway to the emotions of LURVE, as I always discover when the Aforesaid Organ thumps away like a caged tiger whenever I think of DH. How Romantic it is to ponder that if DH's heart were doing the same, it might mean they were trying to fly free of our imprisoning Bods and glide off together into the sunset! Well, it's a Romantic thought until you think of those pix in the medical books Etck, after which the whole idea seems a bit Gross, but it's the Thought That Counts.

HETEROSEXUAL

This means fancying the opposite sex. It is V. Common, which is why there are so many people in the world, and it is what we are all expected to do. It is of course V. Imp to have quite a lot of Heterosexuals on the planet in order to ensure Survival of Species, although some people are saying Gurlz will do it all by themselves one day by a process called parthenogenesis, which apparently is a self-fertilizing method that has worked with cows, and since bulls and cows Doing It looks about as complicated as that thing where twenty-five people stand on each other's shoulders riding a motorbike in the Royal Tournament, I shld think the cows can't wait. Still, since humans find it easier and have maybe worked out more ways to have fun at it, I think this is V. Unlikely to catch on in near future.

Moi, I am a hopeless case, and will not rest until I

have consummated my passion for a Certain Person.
Fortunately I am not a cow (tasteless joke deleted) and
can look forward to V. Graceful and Byootiful
Celebration of our LURVE twenty-five thousand years
from now when DH Sees Sense (sigh, puke).

HOLIDAYS

Scenes of wild romance in stories, but not, in the
humble experience of *moi*, in Real Life. Prob 'cos Brit
beaches (see BEACHES) are full of toddlers, dog poo,
lager louts Etck instead of rippling torsos. Teen
Worriers whose parents whisk them to exotic locations
fare better with gigolos, waiters Etck. There are usually
two of these in any classroom after the summer hols. At

Casualties of the Holiday Romance...

Sluggs, they have time-shares in Tenerife and are immediately recognizable by V. red noses (sunburn) and V. red Eyes (result of copious weeping on account of gigolo, waiter Etck not having written). All I can do is dream of Sun, sand, sea, surf and Sex in distant future with DH.

HOMOSEXUAL: see GAY and LESBIAN

HONEYMOON

My dictionary sez: 'Holiday spent together by newly married couple; initial period of ardour or enthusiasm.' I think it sounds V. Pessimistic, *'initial period of ardour or enthusiasm'* as if you spend a lot of time Doing It, sunning yrselves, dancing the night away Etck on honeymoon and then come back and spend the rest of yr life arguing about why yr partner can't put shelves up straight.

It is thoughts such as these that fritter away countless years of Yoof

I often imagine my honeymoon with DH and I see every moment of it as bursting with ardour and enthusiasm, the ardour the better ha ha. My ideal location for our honeymoon wld be the Moon actually, so no-one cld disturb us for about a hundred years. Doing It might present a few technical difficulties due to weightlessness Etck, but at least saying 'the Moon moved' wld make a change. We cld take a lot of honey, too, for food. This is not as stupid as it sounds, because for once smearing comestibles over yr LURVEr and licking them off might be the only way to avoid dying of starvation. I've seen those space-travel documentaries where they spend the whole flight chasing a piece of toast.

HOPE

Name of LURVE of L. Chubb's Life, and of exotic land where young LURVErs dwell when not wallowing in swamps of jealousy, hurtling into bottomless pits of despair, traversing arid deserts of loneliness, Glume Etck. But how do you maintain Hope when yr Hopes of LURVE may be repeatedly dashed on the Rocks of Fate Etck? Sometimes I think V. Hopeful people are only those with V. Bad Memories who don't remember how often their dreams have Gone Down The Plug.

HORMONES

'Where the whore moans there moan I' as ye ancient
Poet Laureate Scarlett Lady Chubb put it. Hormones
are of course V. Imp things for LURVE, and Teenage
Worrier Hormones are Esp. Active, whizzing about in
Ye Bludde, causing tremors in the Vital Organs Etck.
Hormones are chemicals that make different bits of the
body do things, and not all of them are to do with
Doing It, but to do with ordinary stuff like breathing
Etck. However, I will not concern myself with these
things here, because if you are V. Worried about
Breathing then you maybe need more support than a
modest tome like this can provide. Gurlz sometimes
worry that if they are V. Thin and go up and down in
straight lines instead of in and out in curvy undulations
like Page Three Gurlz, or if they prefer stroking horses'

necks to Boyz' rippling pecs Etck they may be short of vital female hormones, and Boyz sometimes worry that if in their Heart of Hearts they find the thought of stripping down a motorbike more interesting than encouraging Mavis Plume of the Lower Sixth to divest herself of her vest they may also be missing the regulation supply of willy-elevating chemicals. It is usually just a matter of the Right Person having not yet come along and nothing to do with Hormones at all.

HORNY

Boyz use this word to describe how they feel when they have an Overwhelming Need for Fizzical Communion with that special, irresistible and truly spiritual Object of Desire, like all the Gurlz in the back row of the class in turn, their little sister's Barbie, next door's Pomeranian, a jam doughnut Etck. Let it not be thought that the term Horny only applies to Boyz. *Moi* myself have experienced this sensation, ie: an overwhelming urge to Do It NOW.

HORSE

Noble, intelligent beast of great beauty, grace Etck who until V. recently I LURVEd above all things, even Boyz (or espesh Boyz, who all seemed horrible, clumsy,

NB: above, page from my magazine for, about
and BY horses, written when I was twelve...

noisy, ignoble objects by comparison). Hormones have
sadly intervened and put the horse in second place,
although as I have said, I often feel that I wld be
happier burying my head in Dobbin's mane and
galloping through wild fields with carefree wind in
mug Etck than lurking about bike sheds examining
spotz. This is the sad fate of the Inner City Teenage
Worrier who cannot afford riding lessons more than
twice a year and for whom Elysian fields are places with
two blades of grass nourished only by stale urine
sprouting out of the neck of broken lager bottle Etck.

HUG

Aaaaaaah, bless. Away from steamy passions, dear reader, to the warmth of a LURVing hug. A hug is what you give those you LURVE deeply, but not sexually, ie: your ickle brother when he has a bad dream, your cat with the flu, your Granny when she has just knitted you another unwearable item (G. Chubb's latest was a bolero. V. Touching, as she knows I like waistcoats, and I make a point of wearing the purple and orange bolero whenever I see her. Luckily I can easily stuff it in my pocket on way home, as it is several sizes too small, even for *moi*).

A Hug is what you give your Best Frend when she hasn't had a letter from her Malteser for ten days, and it's also (puke time) what therapists tell you to give yourself. I have tried hugging myself many times, and even with long stringy arms like mine it is V. Difficult to get that feeling of being Truly *Embraced* because if you can get yr arms to cross over each other round the back you shld be in a circus anyway and not wasting all this time trying to get therapy on the cheap.

HYMEN

This is the fold of membrane that covers the outside bit of the vagina before a Gurl has Done It, and people used to get V. Excited about wedding nights and hold up bloodstained sheets to prove the bride had been a virgin Etck. This led to quite a trade in false hymens, fake bludde Etck so that the women's husbands thought them pure and didn't abandon them, cut their heads off Etck. In fact, the hymen is usually broken long before a virgin has intercourse, due to horse-riding, vaulting in the gym, tampons Etck, and nowadays hardly anybody realizes they ever had such a thing.

I was going to put HYPNOSIS in here. I am practising it as a last-ditch strategy on D. Hope. But I want to try it on you first, dear reader. Gaze into my eyes... Wooo.... Wooo... Wooo... Wooo... Then, in your own good time, look at page 149...

See? It worked!

CHAPTER SIX
IIIIIIIIIIIIIIIZE to KKKKKKZE

Tonight's the night!

Aggy's flight departs at 21.32 which means I shall probably get my First Kiss with DH at midnight. Swoon, wish I had a glass slipper to drop casually on the runway as I skittishly pretend to flee from his attentions.

As usual on V. Imp occasions, I have the beginnings of a Cold Sore, but I have zapped it with my Wonder Cream which I hope has sent it cowering and snivelling back into the nest of vipers and creepy-crawlies it lives in. I'm going straight round to Spiggs's after school and she will wind the bandages on my leg V. Professionally, and then disguise them under a pair of her mother's V. Natty loose, blue silk trousers.

My only prop will be small bott of TCP and some of Benjy's fake blood to dab on at the last min (it goes a funny colour if you leave it too long). Spiggs advised against this, but she is not too imaginative, coming from a long line of rock breakers. It is V. Kind of her to come with me, though, and she is going to hide behind a copy of **The Telegraph** *(so no-one will know it is her) near the departure lounge, just to check all goes OK. Her mum is V. Kool and says she can stay out till 2 am on Fri nights (grrrr, envy) . . .*

Phew, am scribbling this in the ACTUAL AIRPORT, waiting for a glimpse of my beLURVed. I am V. Glad Spiggy is here as I would have had no idea how to find my way about. We seem to have been going up and down and along on a series of walkways, escalators, lifts and space shuttles for about 45 mins.

Benjy wld love this, but it makes me V. Jumpy. We have stationed ourselves near the check-in for Aggy's flight. It is now 19.00 and she shld have to check in V. soon.

ARRRRRRG. Here she comes!! But where is Daniel? I can't go up to her until he's there, in case he misses her spurning me . . . swooooooooon, I see his golden head. Here goes.

One hour later in the Ladies' loo, Gatwick . . . *It is all going better than I could have dreamed. I rushed up to Aggy and gave her a huge hug and my vast prezzie, telling her not to open it till she gets off the plane (so she won't realize it's a couple of my old jumpers till she is out of Daniel's sight), just as Daniel arrived. I pretended I hadn't expected to see him. V. Kool. Aggy looked distinctly snitty but he was Thrilled to see me and we have all been sharing a coffee ever since and chatting about politics, literature, films and all the things Daniel and I have in common. Naturally, I was being V. Brave, though both of them could tell I was Hiding a Great Sorrow.*

Aggy has been getting more and more grumpy as her precious mins with DH tick away. But I have now tactfully left the love birds (ho ho) as he is going to the check-in with her, and then he's going to wait with her till the plane boards. I pressed my message into his hand as he left. Hope he has sense not to read it in front of Aggy. All I've got to do now is lurk around checking my bandages till He Returns. Gulp. Two whole hours of Agonized Anticipation, which I will nobly fill up with my Alphabet. This Is the Best Moment in my Entire Life So Far . . .

*iiiii*IIIIIIIIIII*iiiiiiiii*IIIII

Ice cream

Ice cream wasn't really associated with SEX in the era of Just One Cornetto Etck, but now we have *Haardon-Arzs*, which it seems you have to eat with no clothes on while entangled in soulful, glistening clinch. Ice cream *is* SEXy because it is V. Slurpy and concentrates yr attention on tongues, lips Etck, and also on thoughts of long, hot, summer days on the beach Etck. What is *not* SEXy about it of course is that it makes you V. Fat and slobby in the end, boo hoo, though not necessarily less LURVable for that of course.

It may be that these new Caring Ice creams are better for you than the stuff that used to be injected with air to make it twice the size (a practice apparently perfected by our long-departed PM Maggie Thatcher in her Mad Scientist student days, and obviously V. Important breakthrough in formulating promises for politicians generally) but I have attempted V. Erotic ice cream-eating pose with extra-slow tongue movements in the presence of various Boyz over recent years, and though it has certainly resulted in some of them reaching hastily for their trousers, this has only been in search of V. Grubby handkerchiefs to gallantly stop the tide of the stuff from drowning *moi*, flooding surrounding countryside Etck. It works for Benjy though; I saw three of his female classmates taking turns to *lick strawberry ice cream off his nose!!!* What is his secret?

What is Benjy's secret?

IDEAS

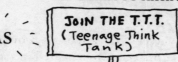

JOIN THE T.T.T.
(Teenage Think
Tank)

Teenage Worriers have V. Excellent Ideas for methods of Saving the World Etck, but when it comes to LURVE Espesh, there is unlimited scope for the wild imagination of Yoof, and we must plumb the depths of our souls to contrive plans, schemes, designs, contraptions Etck for the following:

1. HOW TO MEET PERSON OF YR DREAMZ.
2. HOW TO ATTRACT PERSON OF YR DREAMZ.
3. HOW TO KEEP PERSON OF YR DREAMZ (without padlocks, bondage equipment, wheelclamps, dungeons, suicide notes Etck).

Please send yr ideas to L. Chubb c/o The Publisher so that I can make loads of lolly, er, I mean help the world to be a happier place for Teenage LURVers. Also, lobby the Govt, PM Etck (fill in the form at the back of this book).

Any recipes for LURVE potions, designs for LURVE outfits, ways of making your LURVEr change his mind about *Take That* or your mother Etck, gratefully received.

I also have it in mind one day to do *The Teenage Worrier's V. Imp Ideas Book* which will also include all those Big Ideas that aren't just about LURVE, not that LURVE isn't the Crucial Idea of the Universe Etck.

Just a few Lurve ideas from the
Teenage Think Tank

IGNORANCE

LURVE is blind, it is said, and of course when you are
in LURVE it is easy to remain ignorant of the
drawbacks of yr BeLURVEd even if they are asking you
to lend them yr last penny in the world until their
lottery jackpot money stops being delayed in the post.
But even in LURVE, dear reader, Ignorance is not a
Good Thing because Knowledge Is Power and a Know-
Nothing is often A Victim, like *moi* was when Aggy
Stole My Man (sob, mone, wot a fuel Etck).

Teenage Worriers used to be kept ignorant of the
Facts of Life for as long as possible, but L. Chubb

If only leaflets had V. simple titles like these...

campaigns for an End to Ignorance! Good leaflets
explaining about SEX, reproduction, willies Etck shld
be available at all Secondary schools! Er, I sppose we
cld do Our Bit by not giggling, nudging each other
Etck whenever we get a teacher to answer a tricky
question about SEX, but of couse it can be V. Diff
when they are blushing anyway, and Lechy Lennie in
the back row is whispering loudly that the melon-sized
water bomb he's made out of a condom is filled with
just one shot of his superhuman reproductive materials
Etck.

IMAGINATION

Teenage Worriers have a lot of this, of course, because
Worrying is all about imagining what might happen
but probably won't. You also need it to preserve yr
Self-Respect in the playground, since it's full of people
claiming they've done Incredible, Fearless, Earth-
Moving, Glamorous and Downright Disgusting things
and you need Imagination to work out:

Teenage Worriers soar on the Wings of Imagination...

1) Whether you can get away with pretending the same things.

2) Whether it's anatomically possible to have done the same things or they're just winding you up.

3) Whether you wld get more Self-Respect from cultivating stoical, untainted, cold-shower image in which you use yr Imagination to invent a Higher Plane in which yr Thoughts bubble like a cold, clear spring over spotless pebbles instead of wending their dark and murky way through the oily scum, dropped underwear, and seedy, slithery tendrils of a life Obsessed with Doing It Etck.

I have to say, my Imagination boggles daily at some of the V. Imaginative accounts of encounters with Gurlz that I've heard from some of the Boyz, and I know for sure the only place you find the kind of bazooms they're talking about is on the front of the Sunday Sport and certainly not on any of my Frendz unless they do something pretty clever with a couple of whoopee cushions and keep the lights low.

INDEPENDENCE

What *is* Independence? It isn't living without other people, but I do think it's not living *off* other people. Maybe if I hadn't begged Daniel to promise to stay with me until the Sun turned to a White Dwarf Etck, he might not have got off with my 'frend' instead.

There you are, that's the kind of thing you stoop to when you have no Self-Respect. Since then, I have practised saying, 'you must live your own life, go your own way' to an imaginary DH in the bathroom mirror, and even when I'm *pretending* to do it my cool *femme fatale* smile looks like I've got appendicitis coming on.

L. CHUBB INDEPENDENCE DAY RESOLUTIONS
for when DH is back in my arms:

1) I will keep my own interests alive and spend at least one evening a year with Hazel (talking about DH).

2) I will not wait by phone. I will read Booker shortlist, write postmodern poetry, learn to figure-skate whilst juggling with razor-sharp knives with pool cue balanced on head, and also persuade Adored Parents to invest in portable phone.

3) At parties Etck I will show him I know how to enjoy myself without hanging on to his every word. I will convince some V. Gullible person Also Present that I am a famous journalist writing DH's biography as People's Hero of the Nineties so I can go to the loo alone, but still get a full report on proceedings later.

4) If he wants a night out with the Boyz, I shall not only agree but *insist* that his identity as A Man needs to be periodically affirmed.

5) Must perfect cross-dressing routine, so I can spy – I mean, only to make sure that DH does not come to harm on Boyz' Nights' Out.

Shoulder Pads

V. Big Boots

Must improve cross-dressing technique...

As you know, I am a Feminist and I do think it is V. Imp for both partners to lead full, interesting and Independent lives. When I have got used to Daniel being Mine and only Mine Forever and Ever, I may find I can make this list even more relaxed. See also JEALOUSY.

JJJJJJJ

Jealousy

Aggy knows about The New Fizzics and sometimes goes on about things like Anti-Matter. I think Jealousy is the anti-matter of LURVE. However strong a force yr LURVE is, you can feel exactly the same amount of Jealousy about it, and where LURVE is about Joy, Freedom, Vision, Trust, Optimism Etck, Jealousy is about Glume, Imprisonment, Blindness, Suspicion, Pessimism and lots more I won't go into for fear of causing Mass Suicides Etck.

Pit of despond

DO NOT FALL IN (Lurve)

Lurve is strewn with pitfalls...

I think the Only Answer is to live as full and exciting a life as you can, so that you have other things to think about as well as LURVE and don't look at yr watch all day trying to work out exactly which square centimetre of The World the toe of his left DM would be landing on at just that moment.

L. CHUBB's ROOLZ FOR CONQUERING JEALOUSY:

1) Develop Own Interests and less obsessive hobby than learning how to engrave forged signatures of Ryan Giggs, Stan Collymore, Ian Wright Etck on gold-plated ball and chain made to measure for Him.

2) Do not ask him what he is doing that evening more than twice a day.

3) Do not ring him more than four times a day unless in Dire Emergency (just wanting to hear his voice does not count).

4) Only follow him about in Heavy Disguise (as Cilla Black, John Major, postbox Etck) if having V.V. Good reason to believe he is seeing Someone Else, ie: a Letter arrives for him with unfamiliar handwriting, or he starts wearing his hair differently (on his chest, frinstance).

5) Allow him to kiss other women whenever he likes — viz: his aunt, sister, grandmother, mother.

You can tell I've been reading the right magazines.

JESUS

Jesus talked a lot about the kind of LURVE we wld all like to feel about others and to have them feel for us. He was the Jewish Superhero who inspired Christianity

and preached about turning the other cheek and
LURVing thy neighbour as thyself. This was different
to Ye Olde Testament which went An Eye for an
Eye Etck, wrath, vengeance, better off not in this
world Etck. Although the theory that Life Is Nasty,
Brutal and Short may be more realistic, I prefer Jesus's
version, although there are some neighbours it's hard to
LURVE, like old Mr Spume who is always drunk and
spits food all over you when he talks.

Granny Chubb says 'God is Love' and seems to be
the perfect incarnation of Jesus's way of life. She suffers

V. OLD Specs,
From days
when
EYE TESTS
were FREE

V. Pretty (also
V. stale) biccies
+ dog bics for G.
Chubb

Purse:
Never
contains
more
than £2·30

Another pink
& orange bolero
is imminent...

Granny Chubb walks on water

little children to come unto her, performs miracles like turning half a tin of cat food into a pensioners' banquet, loves her neighbour (Mrs Scragg, who spits on the floor, shares the cat food and never says thank you), scorns money lenders (but wld break open her piggy-bank to buy Benjy sweets), heals the sick (she has more ointments and Mickey Mouse plasters in her medicine cabinet than food in her cupboard) and wld never turn away someone worse off than herself. Maybe she should found a new religion? Anyway, she reckons that if Jesus was alive today he would not get far. Tories would call him a Communist, Lefties wld think he was a New Age Diversionist, Liberals wld say his sell-by date had passed, Style freaks wld ask him where his flares were, New Agers wld say he oughtn't to be so obsessed with his work, vicars wld say he hadn't realized you have to market religion differently now. G. Chubb, however, wld give him a cup of tea and a dog biscuit. See also RELIGION.

JOBS

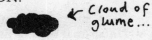 ← Cloud of glume...

Jobs are things some people do all day which they get paid money for. I mention this because lots of Teenage Worriers don't get jobs these days so it's unfair to assume everybody knows what they are.

Naturally jobs are V. imp as you cannot live on LURVE alone and even the greatest pashionne dwindles beside the smouldering embers of the campfire of poverty . . . (I feel a poem coming on).

Teenagers-in-LURVE face a world in which they don't know if they will be able to support their LURVEd ones, little *enfants* Etck.

It's V. Unfair that even at posh places like the BBC, everyone is so scared of losing their own job that they have no time to be generous to young talent (ie: you and *moi*).

Letty Chubb says CAMPAIGN NOW for jobs for Teenage Worriers. We could do useful work for Community half the week, taking old people for walks, wallpapering their flats, painting all those yellowing, pee-stained blocks the councils don't fix, and training to be Cyberspace travellers in the other half.

A few slogans for Teenage Worrier job creation

KANGAROO

The Kangaroo makes history alongside the aardvark in appearing in L. Chubb's guide to LURVE for the simple reason that it carries its ickle babas in a pouch and is therefore a V. Good, Caring, LURVing Mother in the way that I will sadly never be.

KISSING

It is a strange but True fact that one of the things that Worries Teenage Worriers most is How To Kiss. Strange, because most of us have been kissing someone all of our lives and there is hardly a person in the world who does not know that doing an impression of a goldfish with yr lips and fixing them on some unclothed part of Another Person is an Act of LURVE.

There are people who rub noses too, and many of them are Teenage Worriers who have forgotten how to Kiss the minute they are faced with the Object of their Desire.

I am V. Worried about this myself, though, because the Act of Kissing is obv V. Diff from the Art of Kissing and my dreads include the following:

a) Reminding the LURVE object of their dog.

b) Reminding the LURVE object of eating a piece of Ryvita.

c) Reminding the LURVE object of driving a car into a plate-glass window.

(The latter is one of my Biggest Dreads, caused by ill-timed teeth collisions, and resulting in centuries in the dentists' lair, helplessly watching the meter going round.)

Over-eagerness has its drawbacks

It seems V. Weird to *moi* that almost all ickle kiddies are taught to swim (which involves similar breathing dexterity) but no-one gives lessons on how to Kiss. Put Kissing on the National Curriculum say I! What could be more Back To Basics than that? Witness an overnight rekindling of interest in Education Etck among Teenage Worriers!

Anyway, dear reader, please take it from *moi*. When someone you Really LIKE (or really FANCY) kisses you, it comes naturally. It really does! I didn't believe it myself until Daniel and I began to engage in Meaningful Discussions (moan, gnash, will I ever feel like this again) and it was V. Diff from my two other bungled attempts which were like pillow wrestling in mud. Naturally, I haven't had time to experiment much, with tongue-fondling French kissing (maybe it's called French because it's the meeting of two tongues?), or prolonged bouts of soft pecking along upper lip followed by soft pecking along lower lip followed by gentle licking of inside of lips, followed by . . . swooooon. Tragically, Daniel was snatched from me before we had hardly begun. But I have learnt this. It doesn't matter how much you practise on your hand or your pillow; if you get into the right clinch, then it all follows on — but believe me it won't turn your legs to larva (must check spelling before handing this to editor) unless you are kissing the person who is RIGHT for YOU.

(xx)

CHAPTER SEVEN
LLLLLLLLLLLLZ

There's a Greek leg end about a man called Hugh Briss, who, just when he was feeling Over-the-Moon, on Top-of-the-World, Covering Every Inch of the Turf Etck, took a terrible tumble. You won't believe what happened to me.

I waited five hours at Gatwick, dodging hordes of policemen and worrying about bombs. When I realized Aggy's flight really had gone, I scoured the place for DH. Zilch.

At 2 am I remembered Spiggy, who I found asleep under the Daily Telegraph. She had seen nothing of The Beloved either, but was pretty sickened to see moi, as sadly Benjy's fake blood had leaked out and made a V. Nasty mess of her mother's trousers. Another reason people had been giving me a wide berth was that the TCP bottle had broken in my bag, so I smelt like a lavatory. I was now left with the tragic thought that I may have looked and smelt like this while I was chatting so sophisticatedly to Daniel. This did not gladden my drooping soul.

Our return journey was a nightmare, or nitmare as Benjy describes his feelings when our adored Mother is rubbing stuff like battery acid into his head to get rid of wiglice. The worst bit was the unravelling of my bandage, which entwined itself in the escalator, causing a small Security Alert.

Spiggy and I were hoping to creep quietly into her house and lick our wounds Etck but the place was in uproar when

*we got back. My Mother and her Mother were being comforted
by a police officer, assuring them that statistically it was very
unlikely we were both dead and what they usually found in
cases of missing teenagers is that they've only become drug
addicts or gone on the game or got sold into slavery or
something.*

*'What's happened?' I cried in anguish at this scene. I
could only think of one possible tragedy that could have caused
it. 'Don't say it's Da-Da-Da . . .'*

*'No! Nothing's happened to your father, you ungrateful
moron,' yelled my mother, grabbing Wrong End of Stick in
vicelike grip. 'We've been worried sick about YOU!'*

*There is a use for a stutter after all; it can rescue you from
seeming to care more about the Boy of your Dreamz than your
own family, but it was short-lived. Instead of being pleased to
see us, our Mothers rained abuse on our heads, how could we
be so horrible, do we want to get taken into care, don't we
realize the world is full of Junkies, Loonies, Evil Sex
Machines from Hell Etck? This went on for some time,
during which Spiggy and I adopted our usual policy in such
situations of Trying to Think of Something Wonderful, which
in my case was Daniel of course, and in hers, was probably to
do with Maltesers or Bronzed Surfers.*

*What had happened was that Hazel had received a fevered
phone call from Aggy at about 9.30 pm, calling with a V.
Special Message for moi. Knowing I would want to get this
news whilst still hot, Hazel behaved like a Good Pal and
cycled through the Mean Streets of the City Of Shame,
braving the Usual 'Lucky Saddle' Etck remarks from passing
nightime Slaverers and Slobberers to tell me. This went down*

V. Badly with my adored Mother, who thought I was staying at her place. (Moral: Lies will find you out, which is why Macbeth, the well known Scottish serial killer and insomniac kept on bumping off people who knew anything about anything.) Hence the uproar.

But what had Aggy phoned to say? That she was Over-the-Moon, Off-The-Planet, Halfway-to-Paradise Etck because when Daniel went to the check-in desk with her, he sprang a Little Surprise.

He was going with her.

He had done the Romantic Thing and arranged, at the last minute, jeopardizing his 'A' levels, his place in the school cricket team, renewing his subscription to Build Your Own Supercomputer and Everything Else He Held Dear except her, to come with her to Meet Her Mother and Declare his Intentions.

He had packed only his dental floss, a change of underwear and his heart, he said. Per-yuke. And his wallet. Aaargh.

Ecstatic Aggy naturally couldn't wait to tell Hazey Wazey, whose brother is Daniel's Best Friend. So poor, disadvantaged, Brilliantly Brainy Aggy has netted Hearthrob-of-the-Year Daniel Hope. And all because he can afford a plane ticket. For those with dosh, the World is their Oyster.

So all those cops at Gatwick were combing the place for me and Spiggy. Shows you how effective taking cover under a copy of the Daily Telegraph *can be at throwing pursuers off the scent.*

It just shows that even when L. Chubb has just presented him with a written declaration of her intentions to End It

All, he can still jet off into the sunset without a backward glance. I might have been hanging from Spiggy's dad's bandages in the Ladies even as the Big Silver Bird hurtled down the runway. I might have been running screaming into the path of the plane, crying Farewell Cruel World Etck, and he would have felt little more than a slight bump and confused it with the Beating Of His Heart . . . yeech, puke Etck.

I now drift on a grey sea of disenchantment, my horizon limited only by the lowering cloud of GCSEs (yes, the exams, as well as my failure to get enough dosh for Granny Chubb's Spectacles, sob), but otherwise stretching endlessly, drearily, to infinity. An infinity of years, each like the last. Each made of months, weeks, days, hours, minutes, seconds. Each second as long as a year . . .

LLLLLLLLLLLLLLLLLLLLLLLL

LEAP YEAR

INTERESTING FACT: we have Leap Years because the solar year isn't exactly 365 days long. It is in fact 365 days, 5 hours, 48 minutes and 46 seconds long, so there! If you are in LURVE with a Boy Who Wears Anoraks, or if you have a brother of 10, this is the sort of thing they will find V.V.V. Fascinating.

From the Teenage LURVE angle, Leap Years used to be important as the one time a Gurl cld propose

Ho. Hum. Just a little Leap Year practice...

marriage to a Boy instead of the other way round. Liberated Teenage Worriers are above all this of course, and have no fear of proposing in any year (not *moi*, of course, shame, boo, grow up Etck).

LEGS

L. Chubb's LIMB (magnified by factor of SIX ziLLION) →

Gurlz' legs have been the focus of Boyz' lust for centuries. Why? And why doesn't it work the other way round? After all, Boyz' legs also join at a V. Imp place in Gurlz' lives, and they are also usually covered by trousers Etck, but Gurlz do not spend half their lives pretending to drop things to look up trouser legs, following Boyz upstairs, peering through holes in magazines to stare at lower regions of Boyz sitting opposite on trains Etck. This may simply be evidence that Gurlz are generally more civilized.

Of course, Boyz' legs just aren't as *nice*, even I know that, what with knobbly knees, prickly fur Etck. This can be improved on, viz the Alternative Miss World (which is all men in drag) where lots of them look much better than most Gurlz I know, and just goes to show what a razor, slinky tights and a pair of red stilettos can do, moan, whinge.

LESBIAN

Because Queen Victoria apparently didn't believe that women cld be lesbians, SEX between women was never made illegal, so Lesbians have been luckier than Gay men in this respect anyway. But lots of Gurlz are V.

Q: Which of the above is a Lesbian?
A: All... or None... or Some...

Worried about being Lesbian because they don't want to see themselves as being 'like that'. There is still such a strong picture in Society-at-Large (I always think this phrase makes society sound like a criminal) that Gurlz shld have homes and babies, that it is V. Difficult for girlz to admit to *themselves*, never mind anyone else, that they might be Gay.

This means that Gurlz try to hide their feelings and even get up to all sorts of things with Boyz that they really wld rather not do to convince their families (and themselves) that they are straight. Pregnancy, marriage Etck can follow before you've got time to think and a lifetime's unhappiness and yearning unrolls before you.

Of course, crushes can be a passing phase, and at 12 you can fall in LURVE with anyone and wonder why the next day, so it wld be a mistake to assume you know who you really fancy until you are quite a bit older.

If you think that you might be Lesbian, it is V. Imp to try to find someone who you can talk to about yr feelings. You can be almost certain that you know loads of Gurlz and Boyz who feel like you do, but do not trust themselves to admit it in case they are bullied. See also GAY (and Useful phone numbers at the end of this tome).

LETTERS

An essential part of the LURVE affair is the LURVE letter. The great thing about Lurve letters is they stay to comfort you when your beLURVed is far off (or has left, in which case you ceremonially burn them in the garden with yr close friends in attendance, dressed in sackcloth, weeping on each other's shoulders, pledging vengeance, lifelong loathing of Opposite Sex Etck, and then regret it later).

A LURVE-HATE LETTER.

Dear......

I'm writing to say my huge passion for you
is over. In fact my total BOREDOM
grows daily. The more I think of you, the more
tedious you seem. Sadly, the more
I feel this way, so the more I know I must
confess that I really never meant to
ask you to marry me. Our last date proved
there's absolutely no way on earth
I could spend my LIFE with you!
Your revolting habits would depress me.
Being with you would overwhelm me with
misery & glume, and I'd never feel any
happiness, even in the smallest thing.
I know this is cruel, but
I really do mean it. I desperately hope
you accept gracefully and won't say
you long to marry me! You really are
lacking any resemblance to
the marvellous person I first thought.

I can't pretend
I long for your reply

NOW READ IT
AGAIN, LEAVING
OUT EVERY OTHER LINE
Tee hee .....

Also, you can say things in a letter that you might be embarrassed to admit aloud. Although my experience with V. Gorgeous Ken the teacher has proved that paper can be even more embarrassing than the spoken word.

LIPS

Essential item which keeps mouth from consuming all of head, and without which it is hard to talk and impossible to Kiss.

L. Chubb PC make-up Ltd is currently mass-producing lipstick for the masses and working on a V. *Exclooosive* one for the use of L. Chubb and assorted Frendz only (not Aggy). It is flavoured with aphrodisiacs and smells of strawberries. It is also injected with pheronomes, which are not loony-looking plaster garden figures dressed like Egyptian royals but V. Exciting SEXy substances that attract LURVErs though they Know Not Why. See also NOSE.

I am humanely experimenting with these on free-range people, and am hoping to interest Anita Roddick

El.Chubbo's lip-STICK (guaranteed to make his lips STICK to yours...)

NB: El Chubbo's cosmetics tested only on Free-range people

early next year. Incidentally, I think her Body Shops are V. Misleadingly named. If anyone would be able to make good use of a new body it's *moi*, and not only can you not get one but you can't buy a New Body who closely resembles the one who walked out on you for a myopic Brain of Britain either.

Anyway, L. Chubb make-up will be anti-chap (I mean chapped lips, not Boyz) and will stay on lips for at least three hours, unlike Rippoffski Products Etck which smudge on to anything you look at, never mind Kiss.

You may yearn for the bee-stung look but unless you are an LA super-brat and get silicone implants from your parents on yr 12th birthday, you will just have to suffer in silence or smear your lips with honey and stand by a beehive.

See also KISSING.

LOOKS

I've just wasted three hours reading in *HER* (my mother's equivalent of *Smirk*, *Weenybop* Etck that she hides under her pillow) about the return of 'Glamour'. In this learned article, 'dishy' men describe the women they find glamorous and why. All the photos are of luscious LURVElies in Fabu-Bras with jet black dresses, glittering eyes, teeth, jewels Etck. Yet the Dishies also demand 'Sophistication', 'Individuality', 'Dignity', 'Mystery' Etck which they presumably don't extend to the women being Sophisticated enough to say they wouldn't be seen dead with them, dignified enough to say Eff Orff, or Mysterious enough to answer all their queries by playing *Für Elise* on the spoons or wordlessly presenting them with a hardboiled egg with a pink question mark painted on it. Anyway, what use is Mystery in the humdrum life of my darling Mother, frinstance?

Teenage Worrier: Where's my coat/drinking flask/packed lunch/ Etck?

Glamorous Mother. I know not, my darling, and I cannot uncurl from the *chaise longue* to look, alas.

TW: Can't hear you! Have you got a cold?

GM: Surely you don't expect me to take the rose from between my teeth? I'm waiting for your Dishy Father.

TW: But he went out two years ago and hasn't come back . . .

GM: My dignity, allure, mystery, sophistication and indisputable glamour will force him to return, dear daughter. Worry not.

I was V. Worried about this article, because not one of the blokes questioned said he liked a Gurl with no bazooms draped in a grey sweatshirt, black joggers and DMs . . . Is Glamour going to overtake my Designs for the Nineties?? I have an alternative to the return to 'Glamour' with its emphasis on all the traditional bits of Gurlz that make beanpoles like *moi* grind the teeth. Instead of wearing a V. Thin strip accross the middle of your Bod, with Bits bursting out of the top and bottom, why not have shirts stretching from chin to

Sadly, none of the blokes chose the look favoured
by Moi. V. shallow

Lower Bra Zone and skirts from Upper Thigh to
Ankle? Naughty bits on parade. Think how exciting
necks and shoulders wld start becoming if no-one cld
see them! And shins wld be most erotic of all!

Why stop at this? What about total Nudity broken only by EAR MUFFS — the ear may be an erogenous zone already, but it wld become completely irresistible if given this treatment. Or maybe birthday suits plus NOSE COVERS? Then letters to Agony Aunts wld read like this:

Dear Aunty,
I am V. Worried about my nostrils. They are V. Small and thin and make my nose look not so much chiselled, as like a chisel. I have tried to find pictures of normal noses, but my parents hide them all and never let me see theirs undressed. I think my father has some magazines showing Gurlz with noses showing, but they are locked up. I also have a faint greenish discharge from my nose most of the winter. Can you advise?
Yrs,
Desperate (13), Finchley.

L. Chubb Campaign:
Save us all from the Tyranny of Glamour. Otherwise we'll have to drape ourselves around pillars in stilettos, fluttering our eyelashes like our grandmothers had to. A man who truly LURVEs *moi* will take *moi* for what I am. Worry, self-doubt, despair-at-mirror, Will This Do Etck.

I must confess that in a world bombarded with images of Supermodels eight feet tall with legs like a giraffe's and peaches where their Berms shld be, it is hard to keep a Pure Line about such things not

I never get out, never meet anyone new. Just the same four people day in day out. A small fat one who goes to a lot of trouble climbing on a chair to get to see me in the first place then just sticks his tongue out at me. Sometimes I steam up and he writes on me. It is always rude.

There's a grumpy ancient one who slashes himself with blunt blades and then curses at ME as though it's MY fault and another old one who only gazes mournfully and sighs. But the worst is a stringy individual who poses for HOURS, holds up other mirrors trying to see her profile as if I'm not doing my job properly, examines her plukes in excruciating close-up, and ponces about trying out faces, voices, hairdos while the rest of her family are trying to break the door down.

I had a better time when I was working for that loopy old Queen that banged up Snow White. At least she talked to me.

Just as well Mirrors can't talk. This is what ours would say.

mattering and stop posing about in front of a mirror for weeks on end.

L. CHUBB'S TIPS:

1) Learn to LURVE yr Bod. Remember, you've got more or less the same bits as Supermodels, only in some cases (Nose, Berm, Ears, Spots Etck) probably larger, but this may also go for yr brain, and thus make you more likely to write yr own autobiography Etck.

2) Bear in mind that even V. Beautiful people get old and by the time they're 50, everyone looks much the same unless they are V. Rich and have face-lifts. Then they look like Cats when somebody's just let off a firecracker, and they have to have their cheekbones taped to the back of their necks and their foreheads pulled over the back of their skulls like half-peeled tomatoes, which looks V. Odd.

3) Girlz who are beeeeyooootiful miss it V. Much when it goes away. A Happy old face is nicer than a grumpy old face. Also, they have less to fall back on, having never had the time to even read a book as they have been too busy fighting off blokes and deciding what to wear.

4) Do not consider *your* appearance to be any more important than a *Boy'z* appearance.

I know I go on and on about how V. Handsome Daniel Hope is, but I like to think I wld LURVE him even in a diff shape, when he is fat, bald Etck. It is his SOUL that interests me (noise of throat clearing, self-justification, lie detector exploding Etck).

LUCK

It is lucky to be born rich, beautiful or clever, but those with these advantages do not always sustain them. Then they become unlucky, which is one of life's Paradoxes.

If you're lucky in LURVE it means you happen to be in the room when the Only Person in the World who is Perfect for You walks in. Obviously you cld spend 80 years on the planet without this happening, so most of us make do with the nearest available person who's willing and doesn't have too many odd habits like fartlighting in Tesco's checkout, fancying Kylie Minogue Etck, though even these things have undoubtedly formed the foundations of many Wonderful Partnerships. This puts romantic LURVE firmly in, um, context, I think.

Being Unlucky in LURVE means meeting said person and finding they are a) already married, b) enjoy a bit of light axe murdering, Etck. I carry my Lucky Rabbit's Foot (remember, animal lurvers, it is not a *real* rabbit's foot) at all times in an attempt to stave off Dame Fortune's bitterest blows and have always believed that the reason Daniel went off with Aggy (on that fateful night recounted in my previous tome) was because I had abandoned the rabbit's foot for an evening as I was trying to look slinky, and wherever I put it, it made a bulge.

LURVE

What is LURVE? This book is all about LURVE, and yet I am V.V. Worried that I still don't know what this strange, scary, stormy, wonderful force is, or whether Deep True Lasting Lurve is possible for two human beans (unless they were Granny and Grandpa Chubb, sob).

Could LURVE just be Nature's trick to keep the human race going? sob, worry...

Cats, too have their passions

Teen Worriers believe it's the most important thing on Earth. I hope we're right.

See also LUCK, LUST, ROMANCE, WILLIES, Whole of rest of BUKE, Etck Etck Etck Etck.

LUST

Lust is when yr Bod goes into meltdown at the sight or thought of a particular person, but one who need not necessarily be a LURVE object. Boyz' Willies especially can leap up and start squawking for company even in the presence of the odd missing shirt-button or visible bra-strap, even when the poor Boyz are thinking about something quite different, like scoring off a scissors-kick from a Ryan Giggs pass, or which way round the left threaded sprocket-widgeter goes back on a 1987 Ford Catastrophe.

Lust and LURVE, in a perfect world, go hand in hand (ahem). But each is possible without the other. My relationship with Rover is free of lust, frinstance, and my wince-making hots for Brad Pittbull were, I now see, free of LURVE so don't be fooled that Gurlz don't feel it too. It can at these times be V. Diff to distinguish between Lust and LURVE and if my ancient parents are anything to go by, the loss of one has a knock-on, or rather knock-off effect on the other, or The Other.

It may be that the only way to keep both alive is to meet your True LURVE about once a year in a Spesh room full of soft music, silky bedclothes, purple drapes, cascading fountains, truckloads of roses Etck, and avoid doing anything dreary like washing up, putting cat out, changing nappies Etck together. What this means

Environment in which Lurve & Lust will endure...

for the future of the nuclear family is unclear, but since unclear and nuclear are anagrams of each other, perhaps langwidge is trying to tell us something we shld have known for centuries.

And in which it won't...

LYING

What Boyz do when they say they will LURVE you for ever and how cld you possibly think all they want is your body when they worship your Very Soul, but are in such an agony of desire that they will kill their Selves if you do not succumb to their undying passion to have All Of You. Also when they say: just let me share your bed, I won't do anything. Also when they say, don't worry, I won't come inside you, which is what Jackie Stoat who used to be in the Fifth Year is always warning anybody who'll listen when her baby gives her five seconds off from yelling so she can get the words out.

Translation: Don't tell my wife

CHAPTER EIGHT
MMMMMMMMMMMMMMMZE

*I was wrong. The days DO drift aimlessly by. But they are
littered with ludicrous events that make one ponder the awful
possibility of God as a V. Bad stand-up comic who has failed
audition in other dimension and ended up with V.V. Low
Budget show called The Human Race.*

*My Adored Father had fixed the plumbing following the
unfortunate incident with the drill and the dinosaur, and on
Sunday it unfixed itself. Nobody realized this at first.
Everyone was V. Pleased that Benjy was being so quiet in the
kitchen playing with Horace, be thankful for small mercies
Etck. It was only when my Only Mother took a close look into
Horace's cage that she found he was floating, V. Depressed, in
V. Yukky pool of poo, gerbil pellets, bits of Guardian Etck in
a half-shredded paper boat made by Benjy, who was looking
on V. Proud.*

*Benjy was trying to see how long it took Horace to eat his
transportation and showed no interest in where the Straits of
Horace had suddenly come from. 'Water,' Benjy eventually
declared firmly, pointing at the ceiling. A steady trickle was
coming through the plaster and dripping through the bars of
Horace's abode.*

*My father still refused to call a plumber, which slowed
repairs to the point where we all ended up having to sleep in
the same room for two nights of torture, and Benjy dreamt*

*Captain Nemo had driven his submarine into our back yard
and had wrapped him in seaweed and cooked him as a
delicacy. At least he kept my adored parents awake, not just
me for a change. His kitten has given Rover fleas. The rest of
us, too.*

*My father says it's impossible to work in this madhouse
and my mother says, what's new? I am not allowed out in the
evenings because of the airport incident and my entire Granny
Chubb Fund has gone on Dry-cleaning Spiggy's Mother's
trousers. I have written a furious letter to Freak-Your-
Granny Novelties PLC, complaining they've no right to make
fake blood for kiddies that doesn't wash out. These joke
manufacturers are obviously in League with Dry Cleaners;
one day I will establish the connection by combing the records
at Companies House like they do on those V. Serious
documentaries where the reporters talk as if their trousers are
on fire.*

*My mother is off to her horrible mother's for a week to
paint and Find Herself, leaving me to cherish her only ickle
Benjy. And at half-term, too. At least he does care about me
and it gives me a chance to wander soulfully about the parks
and playgrounds yearning for my Lost Youth, now sunning
himself in the West Indies, grrrr, yearn, wince. At night,
Benjy and I share our nightmares, shivering in our lonely
garret. Mine are all about planes crashing and I wake up
trying to find my life-jacket under the bed. True Lurve will
not die, even when it has been so cruelly betrayed.*

*Unopened bills are piling up and my father is retreating
further into a New Age fantasy mode where he seems to think
we can survive if only we can learn to Love Each Other. But*

he has forgotten the Magic Ingredient: Love is more than just smiling sweetly when your Life Partner floods the house.

I have seen True Lurve shine from Rover's eyes, so our house is not entirely barren of it. And that is when they are fixed on her unopened tin of Kitty Bliss . . . I bury myself in my work. If I can never be happy, then at least I can Help others be miserable too . . .

MMMMMMMMMMMMMMM

Just ONE week's supply of mags, papers Etck. at our house →

MAGAZINES

If we had been Teenage Worriers a couple of centuries ago, we wld have had much less to Worry About. And this is becos we wld not have been made so V. Neurotic by Magazines.

When I am Prime Minister I will ban *Smirk, Weenybop, Tru-Luv, Yoo-hoo* Etck so that no-one has to waste precious days and weeks poring over advice about how to make their eyes, bazooms and lips bigger while minimizing their stomachs, bottoms and hooters. No-one will yearn for glitter eyeshadow, stop-wrinkles-from-starting Wondercreams, hairpieces, How To Please Their Man in 5,000 zillion positions Etck Etck.

All you need, dear reader, is this humble tome and the Karma Sutra plus plenty of practice, which you will not get reading soppy stories about soap stars, or even

Ye Wicked Worlde is out to confuse Teenage Worriers...

fab pop stars in daft magazines. And think, if you didn't buy all those mags, how much Richer you'd be. And how much happier too. Unless you can break this Habit now, it will last into Old Age, eg: my adored Mother can still get into a rage when she compares the Superlux kitchens in *HER* or *Tittler* to the collapsing packing cases with handles that come off in yr hand that my Adored Father has 'fitted'.

Anyway, here followeth a sample of the headlines of one of the lower grade Mother's Magazines that you might be saddled with if you can't kick this habit now (NB This is just ONE issue):

ALL I ATE FOR A YEAR – Bread, Butter & Chocolate
I'M 14, MUM'S 37, Guess who's the Model?
MY GUILT I've Blown Our Savings
CELLULITE – 12 Things You Need to Know
58 cooking tips and recipes
THEY USED TO CALL ME UGLY (accompanied by pic of V. Famous V. Beautiful Gurl)
WIN £10,000 CASH

My New Year Resolution next year will be to Ban Magazines from my Life. Meanwhile I shall cut down gradually by buying just two or three a week instead of five. (Must get that one that says 40 tips on how to get your boyfriend back, though . . .)

MAKE-UP

El Chubbo's cosmetic range soon to be launched (see also LIPS) in The Face Shop, where, if you are V. Rich, you will be able to buy a completely new off-the-peg (Worry shld this be off-the-neck?) face. El Chubbo's cosmetics *Guarantee* a lifetime's perfect complexion, eyes bigger than Bambi's, a wig fuller than the Lion King's, lashes that you'll need to protect from onslaughts of sexually aroused spiders thinking their beLURVed has rolled over and is awaiting them on yr lids, lips whose lustre will never dim, Etck. You will also be able to buy yr beLURVed a new face, that will

be programmed to kiss, intone werds of LURVE on command Etck. I hope the Advertising Standards Authority will allow me to get away with this modest series of claims for my inventions. I expect so.

MARRIAGE

Wrongly thought (if divorce statistics are anything to go by) to be happy culmination of Romantic Lurve. Arg. See AISLE, ENGAGEMENT, FIANCE, WEDDINGS Etck. That's enuf about marriage.

MASTURBATION

This is what you do in the privacy of your own room if you are lucky enough to have one. The bathroom is the other favourite venue as long as it's got a good lock. Masturbation is basically Doing It with yourself (all, tragikly, that I will ever do . . .), and therefore certainly has some limitations re Survival of Human Race Etck. But though a lonesome pleasure, it is a V. good way of getting to know what kind of things your body likes. Lots of Teenage Worriers feel V. Embarrassed and ashamed about it as though it's a Bad Thing to do.

It isn't, of course. It doesn't make you Blind or mad, which a lot of people used to think, but it also (so I am told, ahem) is not so interesting as Doing It with someone else. It is a V. Good way to get started

however, and much better than practising on a person
with whom you have nothing else in common and with
whom you might feel Deep Regrets. See also
CLITORIS, WILLY Etck.

My publisher has demanded that instead of
the above, I draw a bunch of flowers
for you to give yourself...

MEETING

It is Surprising, in these days of co-education and
Freedom Etck, that a big Worry of lots of Teen
Worriers is still How to Meet a Boy or Gurl. This is
partly because it is so V. Embarrassing to fall in Lurve
with someone in the same school as you that most of us
avoid it like the plague and treat even the most
fanciable people in our class as just Good frendz. Also,
when you sit next to someone all day and notice them
picking their nose, belching Etck it does diminish
Mystery (rather like marriage seems to, sigh).

Across a crowded room with yr eyes strung on a twin
beam and yr hearts palpitating in unison is prob the
best kind of LURVE meeting, but is V. Rare, even for
Teenage Worriers who think they are falling in
LURVE every five minutes. Parties are still the best
places to find this situation, as pubs, clubs Etck are
likely to be filled with puking, raves, wall-to-wall
football on TV, quiz nights Etck. But even at parties (if
you have the courage to go in the first place) you have
to have a few chat-up lines handy (see BANTER), or
else the brazen ability to spill yr drink down his T-shirt
and hope he'll enjoy the mopping up.

Hazel always said museums and Art Galleries were
V. Good pick-ups for intellekshuals like *moi*, and frendz'
brothers are also V. Good (ie: I met Daniel because he is
Hazel's brother's Best friend. Moan, will-I-ever-see-his-
like-again?). Your parents' friends' V. Accomplished
teenagers are no good. ('But Letty darling, he's a genius

at maths, and they're saving a job for him in his father's accountancy business. Can't you bring yourself to at least go to the cinema with him?')

LETTY CHUBB'S GUIDE TO HOW TO MEET LURVE PARTNERS

oops!

1. Lurk by Bus Stop till you spot Person of Your Dreams
2. Board Bus
3. Scatter loose change in Lurve Object's lap

Alternatively, wait for snow. It is V. Romantic to meet in Winter Wonderland

... Do not wait forever

NB V. Imp tip for boyz: If a Gurl is walking alone at night, never walk on same side of street as her, always cross over so she will not feel threatened. It is V. Scary walking alone. Advice to Gurlz: If you ever do feel some creepy creep is following you, don't be embarrassed, just RUN. Better safe than sorry Etck.

MENSTRUATION: see PERIODS

MONOGAMY

Only Doing It with one person, which leaves a lot to be desired (arf arf yeech). If I COULD just get a chance to do it with one person then at least I cld find out if Monogamy is the right lifestyle for *moi* . . .

MONA LISA

For centuries, blokes have adored V. enigmatic images of women. Greta Garbo in films, Mona Lisa in paintings. 'What is she thinking?' they ask themselves. And 'Is that special smile for me alone?' Nuts. Greta Garbo has said that she was asked by directors to make her mind a blank. Mona Lisa clearly does not wish to reveal she has V. Few teeth, a common Worry in those days. (Avocado da Vinci, incidentally, is another good example of a V. Clever Gay Artist.)

MOON

The moon in June is for mooning over with yr one True LURVE. But, byootifull as it may be, I have often wondered why a barren wasteland of craters, ash Etck shld be the star of so many LURVE songs. Full moons put me in mind of wolves and periods.

Benjy does not find the moon romantic...

MOTH

A moth caught in a flame: *moi* in the light of Daniel's gaze. Sob.

MOTHER

LURVE begins on Mama's knee; the Hand that Rocks the Cradle Rules the World. L. Chubb's theory is that Teenage Worriers and their Darling Only Mothers are best separated for looooong periods.

This is because, although Mutual LURVE is undeniable, with it comes a panoply of Anxiety, eg: Perfectly normal Teenager is behaving in perfectly Normal way (picking nose, sleeping till midday, gazing soulfully at wall, TV Etck. Moping in festering room, unable to lift finger). Perfectly Normal Mother is also behaving in Perfectly Normal Way (going up wall, asking 'where did I go wrong', making lots of helpful suggestions: 'why don't you play the piano/do some drawing/comb your hair/get dressed any more' Etck).

where did I
go wrong?

DOOZE

R Parent

offspring

It will be obvious to a detached observer that these two behavioural types are unsuited to the same habitat. Mothers and ickle daughters are fine. Mothers and grown-up daughters are V. Good frendz (often). But Mothers and Teenage Worriers Do Not Mix. See PARENTS for HINTS and TIPS.

MUSCLES

Boyz are always messing around with their Biceps, flexing them in front of mirrors, pumping iron, jogging, huffing and puffing Etck. Most Boyz stop longing for them when they are about 25 (and have given up all hope of being Batman Etck).

A bit of bicep looks nice, but I am trying to suppress

Gurlz have biceps too...

it as a well-developed, rippling SOUL is so much more important. Also, re the BAZOOM Dept, a Boy without a Bicep is just as Important a Person as a Gurl without Big Bits Etck. Of course, in a fair, equal and just Universe, there wld be bicep pads for Boyz, just like padded bras, though V. Scrawny legs and forearms with Arnie Schwarzenegger torso might look a bit Strange. BAZOOMZ, after all, are only expected to live in one place.

MUSIC

If Music be the Food of LURVE, play on, said the Famous Bard W. Spokeshave. And 'Our Song' is a V. Famed ingredient of LURVE's sweet soup, leading to canoodling or weeping whenever its haunting strains (or straining haunts, in case of Brian Bolt) waft in Summer air. I feel a poem coming on . . .

Jazz is a particularly Fashionable type of music with such good connections with LURVE that the story goes

Ye human race is united by ye Music of
THE BLOBES...

the word 'jazz' originally meant Doing It. Jazz can be
V. Romantic and Smoochy, allowing you to dance V.
Slowly and As One with yr LURVer, it can be V. Fast
and Jumpy so you can flail yr lissom limbs about and
work up Big Sweat, or it can be V. Intense and Weird
so you can look into yr LURVer's eyes and go, 'I wish
we knew how to LIVE that much'. The thing about
Jazz musicians is that like people in LURVE, they
catch the moment and spin it until it is a fiery blur,
phew, pant, perspire Etck. The right Music is a V. Imp
part of yr LURVE armoury, so choose with care . . .
(obv Daniel did not appreciate my True LURVE of the
music of *The Blobes*. But I know I shall prove him
wrong, and when they are No.1, remember you read it
here first, Regret, Doom Etck).

CHAPTER NINE
NNNNNZ, OOOOOOOOOOOZE, PPPPPEEEEEEEEEZE

Unbelievable! An Express Letter from Daniel! I tremble:

Dearest Scarlett,

I have made a terrible mistake. Seeing you at the airport made me realize your true calibre.

To have come all that way, racked with pain from an injury you were too brave to mention and in anguish over an Unnamed Sorrow, to see off a friend who had not yet learned how to care, was an act of such faith, such courage, such ineffable sweetness, that I felt once again the great surge of Love for you that I so cruelly turned my back on.

Scarlett, forgive me, I was in despair. I had promised myself that I would help Aggy through the searing reunion with her mother, but know, in my heart, that my Past, Present and — dare I say it? — Future, lay only with you.

Letty, Letty, Letty, darling. Can you ever forgive me?

We were made for each other.

Aggy understands.

I have tried to telephone you from the four corners of the Globe. I am flying back on Friday. I beg you, if you will, to meet the flight . . .

Then he gives the flight details Etck and goes into some

descriptions of my bod (including parts he hasn't even seen — yet) in glowing detail. Modesty forbids repetition. Need I say how I feel? I'll be at Gatwick at 1600 hrs on Fri. I forgive you Daniel, yes, yes, a thousand times yes. Oh, how the wheel of fortune spinneth . . .

NNNNNNNNNNNNNNN

NAILS

I am not a supporter of the Ðaft belief that scarlet talons turn Boyz to abject, pleading, subservient jellies Etck.

First, you spend centuries growing them, filing them with something that looks as if it sharpens road-drills, paint them with stuff they spray cars with, then inhale noxious gases from the antidote whenever you try to get rid of them. Catwoman I am not. Vampires, *femmes fatales* Etck will not agree, but Yaa boo to them is what I say, another e.g. of L. Chubb's scintillating wit, repartee Etck.

NECKS

Kissing used to be called Necking in old black-and-white American movies, but of course if two people try

to kiss each other with their Necks it can be V. Awkward and may even require prolonged physiotherapy later. The Neck, however is V. Important for Nuzzling, an essential LURVE move.

My own, sadly, falls into giraffe category and although I have walked around with piles of my Adored Father's encyclopaedias on my head before they were reclaimed by the HP company, it does not seem to have either improved my posture or shortened my neck. I have put this Worry on my list of Plastic Surgery Operations for when my Ship-comes-In and meanwhile make vain attempt to comfort myself with knowledge that at least it means I have a longer erogenous zone (my neck is V.V. Sensitive).

NIGHT

Most SEX occurs at night in bed (see BED) say experts, which just shows they don't ask Teenage Worriers.

Most Teenage Worriers' Doing It experiences occur in afternoons in parks, pretending to do homework together while Adored Parents have *EastEnders* on V. loud downstairs Etck.

I wld qu like my First Time to be at night however, or at least in late afternoon winter powercut, as I am V. Shy of anyone (even DH, swoon – or espesh DH) seeing my mangy frame in glare of floodlights. I wld, however, suffer Big Worry of wondering whether he LURVed me for myself or whether he was pretending I was Jackie Cumming from Page Three. I guess the best thing wld be Total Blackout for body area combined

with craftily poised low light for lips and eyes, Etck, so you cld be quite sure you were Doing It with person of yr Choice and not their frend who they had sent in for a Dare. A Worrier's Imagination is a fevered thang.

NIPPLES

Pointy bits on end of breasts that are common to both sexes but are focus of absurd degree of interest for Boyz. Presumably they never got enough of this ickle item when they were babas. Well, I do not blame them for this, but if only they cld keep a sense of proportion and see that staring at Nipples Etck can be V. Embarrassing for the owner of same.

Boyz treat Nipples like light-switches – fiddle with them and electricity immediately courses through Gurlz' Bods, making Earth Move Etck. Well, in my humble experience (confirmed by the luxuriously-endowed woman-of-the-world Hazel also), a neck or a shoulder can be equally erogenous and a better prelude to Doing It than being made to feel you are a kind of human arcade game that just needs to be twiddled and pressed for Bonus Points. Also, if you have resorted to stuffing a few tissues down yr bra to increase yr allure, you will find it V. Diff if a nipple-freak gets to the points before you've had time to go to the Ladies . . .

Teenage Worriers ask, are my nipples *normal*? Apparently there are so many diff kinds (pink, brown, beige, huge, invisible to all but electron microscopes, pointy, inverted, Etck Etck) that almost anything is normal, including V. Hairy ones. I have tweezed out the odd hair myself, blush.

NO

This word is V. Good Value. For just two little letters, cunningly adjacent in alphabet and therefore easy to recall, it should make sure you don't get what you don't want.

USE IT.

The papers are always full of stories (usually V. Upsetting reports of Rape or Harassment cases) where Boyz say they thought the Gurl really meant 'yes' though she said 'No', which shows there is still much work to be done. It is V.V. Imp to say 'No' whenever anyone touches you ANYWHERE you're not comfortable with, whatever they may say about it.

'No' can sometimes mean 'not now', 'try again next week after you've brushed your teeth/changed your socks/I've got rid of this nine-foot pluke' Etck. But in order to Grow Up (writhe, Worry, will I ever learn to do this, what is it anyway Etck?), Gurlz must also learn to accept that No means No and not hang around mooning after their Teenage True LURVE has family of four, Etck.

No NO no NO no NO NO NO

NOBEL PRIZE

When I am World leader, guided by the Advice of the Teenage Think Tank, I will award a Nobel prize FOR LURVE. It will not go to a Lothario or a Don Juan, but rather to a V. Noble good soul like Granny Chubb, who LURVEd and was LURVEd and lived V. Quietly doing the best she could. Sigh.

NOSE

My attempts to redesign this Bodbit have failed miserably but I feel that those of us with V. Big ones shld Speag Owd re our improved respiration, noble profiles Etck. Stand Up for big Hooters! Stage the Alternative Nose Beauty Parade, or The Nose Show on TV. Big Nose Campaigners cld take to the streets! (Council operatives with bogey-scoopers cld follow if the objection was the public health risk.) As you see, this is a sore point with *moi*, and with my Cold Prob it's often a pointed sore as well.

V. Imp Nose Fact: our noses can spot pheronomes, tiny chemicals that float about without us being aware of them consciously. However, they may well affect our behaviour as they are supposed to be powerful sexual attractants. Phew.

Noses can spot pheronomes, so the bigger the better

NOSTALGIA

What LURVE is to Middle-Aged Worriers who believe it is All over For Them. Some deal with this by rushing off into second and third marriages to recapture Old Magic, bor-ing, puke Etck, some wander about listening to old music and feeling sorry for themselves. I wonder if I am a Middle-Aged Worrier in a Teenage Worrier's spindly form sometimes, as I have been nostalgic ever since I was about 7 years old. I get this feeling V. Badly in Autumn when I see fogs and drifting smoke and think of Summer passing with all the joys it didn't bring (whinge, violins, pull-self-together).

only the Best in El Chubb's library

TOLSTOY · Dickens · BRONTE · TONI MORRISON · J. Austen · T. HARDY · George Eliot

V. IMP. BOOK

NOVELS

Reading can be V. much better than Real Life...

V. Good for Romantic Teenagers-in-LURVE to wallow in. I stick with the classics (it took me three years to get through *Age of Innocence* and *Middlemarch* so I'd forgotten the beginnings after a bit, but I Felt A New Person At The End, unfortunately they ran away screaming, arf arf, groan). However, I do not feel that reading Daft Romances will attract the attentions of the cleft-chinned interllekshual Wunderbabe for whom you are searching, dear reader(s).

OOOOOOOOOOOOOOOOOO

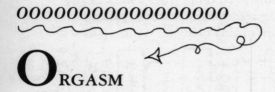

ORGASM

The climax of LURVEmaking is supposed to be the Orgasm, that Liquefying of the Loins, Volcano of Ye Vitals, Explosion at the Extremities, Etck that . . . wait a minute, must run cold shower and consult Dictionary for more sober advice, viz: *violent excitement, rage, paroxysm; climax of sexual excitement esp. in coition.*

Well, I don't think much of that, even though I know I'm dancing in the dark on this subj., since my knowledge of Orgasm has so far not been in a two-player game, as t'were. But it seems V. Typical of adults that they wld describe this LURVEly feeling as a rage or paroxysm, but maybe the dictionary compilers are among the many adults who, apparently, have never

Others suffer inadequacy and glume saying:
will I ever have an orgasm? I suffer, saying:
will I ever DRAW one?

experienced Orgasm. Most of these are women, because
it is only necessary for most Boyz to perform a Willy
Action similar to pumping a bicycle tyre to experience
Orgasm (see EJACULATION) and Gurlz are made
differently so their Bods often have to be guided to this
V. Pleasant state by more roundabout routes.

It does presumably Stiffen The Resolve (even more
heh heh, arf arf, Carry On Willies Etck) of Boyz V.
Worried about their working parts to feel that they are
making a Gurl Go Wild With Pashion Etck just
through the Masterful Movements of the Member, and
portrayals of Gurlz Doing It in magz and movies often

have a lot of this panting, wailing Etck, and stuff that would make me go out for an asthma inhaler before I tried it again.

Gurlz shld not be too Worried if they don't feel like this, even with a Boy they LURVE, because we all experience SEX differently, like everything else that happens to us. Hazel, after all, says she wasted a lot of breath carrying on like this with Boyz but really only felt it when she discovered Gurlz, which shows it doesn't have to have anything to do with Proud Members Etck or any of that rubbidge.

People say it is poss to have a v. long happy LURVing life without even discovering Orgasm at all. I hope this will not apply to *moi*, though, as I believe you are likely to have a longer and happier and more LURVing life if you do.

ORGIES

This means lots of people all doing it together. I am too Worried about AIDS Etck. Also too shy.

PPPPPPPPPPPPPPPP

PARENTS

It's well-known that most Teenagers think their parents are fools. By the time the Teenager has reached

20, they are surprised to see how much their parents have learned in just six years.

As demonstrated above (see MOTHERS), El Chubb's theory is that Parents and Teenage Worriers shld only be allowed Limited access to each other, since during these Difficult Years they can often give each other a V. Hard Time. Teenage Worriers usually want the deal with Parents to be as follows, ie: that is, viz: To provide Food, Laundry, Shelter, Dosh, Listening Ear Once a Week.

Sadly, Teenage Worriers keep finding themselves being buried under piles of moaning, festering, shrieking Worries dumped on them uninvited by their elders.

Parents are unable to keep their Wandering Minds off their V. Great Anxieties re Edukashun, Appearances, Behaviour Etck for long enough for the Teenagers in their lives to consume nosh, change clothes Etck that they are supposed to provide. Hence ye beLURVed Family (see FAMILY), instead of being Bastion against Cruel World, refuge from alien Universe Etck, becomes claustrophobic Vipers' Nest in which it is impossible to pick nose and play Chumbawumba records in peace. This will change (I am told). Meanwhile, here are some strategies for surviving:

1) Think: My Mother's nagging is Normal. She only Does it 'cos she Cares.

2) Ask to go on foreign Exchange to Moon Etck for a break.

3) Make lists of 'dos' and 'don'ts' for yr mother. Reward her with nice smiles, early nights Etck when she follows them.

4) Be sure to set clear boundaries so she knows what you will and will not allow.

5) Talk to other Teenage Worriers with similar probs – it's a relief to Find You Are Not Alone.

6) Remember, your mother will grow out of it by the time you are 75.

See also MOTHER, FAMILY.

PARTIES

Where smooching Etck so often begins and leads on to Things You Regret. At least, that's how the story goes . . . Anyway, every time there is a hint of one I get all V. Excited. This is going to be the Big Night.

It usually takes me a few weeks of Worry before deciding what to wear. When I have finally picked just the right shade of grey sweatshirt and chosen which of the five fab colourways I will use for trousers (the L. Chubb range includes: Jet black, Bat Black, Coal black, Pitch black, Sable, Ebony and Shadow) I will feel that familiar tingling feeling. Is it the prospect of meeting the One I LURVE? Or the Thrill of seeing that I have transformed at last from Ugly Duckling to Swan? No, it is the start of a cold sore.

If you are Worried by Parties, you are Not Alone. I have decided that every party-giver shld keep a small corner with comfy chairs, magz, twiglets Etck for those who are shaking too much to walk and too shy to talk.

PENIS

As the reader of my other great work will already know, I find this word V. Scratchy and do not like the way it is an anagram of 'snipe' and 'pines'. And 'spine'. A few thousand years with a Freudian wld perhaps cure *moi* of this. Meanwhile, I'll use 'Willy'. See WILLY.

PERFUME

Daniel gave me perfume once. He tarnished this beautiful gesture by remarking how much more expensive it was than the last time he bought it. This led to my emotions alternating between gratitude, seething jealousy of whoever he'd bought it for last and a nagging feeling that under the dazzling exterior lay a hint of parsimony.

I smelt like a flowershop for two wonderful weeks, then Benjy mixed my precious bottle with shaving foam, washing up liquid, shampoo and turpentine to make a Potion. Potions are so popular with 5-10 yr olds that the toy business is now making a fortune selling Green Slime, Creeping Yukkk, Brown Spume

Some will sink to low tricks...

It's Eau de Goalpost

BOYZ! Wear THIS and attract MOI!

Parfum de FUDGE

... but not moi

Etck. Amazing to make money out of stuff that even the poorest people can find in their hankies any time they want. Anyway, this does not stop small maniacs like Benjy from hijacking ingredients like my precious Perfume.

Interesting that Boyz' perfumes are always leather, spice, woodland Etck while Gurlz' are all flowers and things. But why not choose food? Parfum de Profiteroles? Or Eau de Yorkshire pud? I wouldn't mind sending Aggy some Boiled Sprout cologne . . .

PERIODS

All a period is, is the womb getting rid of the unfertilized egg that you have started producing. This means that periods are, of course, closely related to LURVE because without them there would be no babies. Lots of Teen Worriers waste vistas of time Worrying that their periods haven't started yet. I know many of you are still waiting – I waited long enough, and bought four hundred packets of tampons in the process, eventually discovered and savaged by Rover who thought they were white mice.

Now my Periods are here I can tell you I regret counting the days Etck. Take advantage of your yoof while you can, for it fleeeth quickly and if your best Friend started at 11 she was V. Young. Lots more Teen Worriers, even in today's Modern World, do not know exactly what a period is, and are V. Worried they will suddenly gush blood whilst going upstairs in front of The Most Wonderful Boy In The World Etck. I wore press-on pads for years with this fear in mind, but do not worry, they do start qu. gently and you will almost certainly feel it. Some people still think they cannot get pregnant if they have sex during their Period. They CAN. So can YOU. (Dire warning, condom, Etck.)

Rover stalks the tampons...

PERSONALITY

What makes a Person a Person, the definitions more or less say. That's a big help isn't it? Plukes, and legs like uncooked spaghetti are part of what makes *moi*, L. Chubb too, but they're not my Personality – still, I suppose they have an *effect* on my Personality by making me fraught, shy, self-loathing Etck, little self-image probs like that.

Only a Fule wld think Personality has nothing to do with yr Bod, since the way that Nature has chosen to hang yr particular bits and pieces together has a V. Big

effect on the way you walk and talk and wave yr hands
about Etck.

However, what people usually mean when they talk
about Personality is the stuff people do that makes you
remember them. If yr Impact on The World is such
that everybody wonders where that faint whirring noise
is coming from when you talk, stick wallpaper on you
Etck, it means you need to work on yr Personality.

Some Personality exercises for LURVE situations:

1) *Eyes*. Eye contact is V. Good for establishing
rapport with others, makes them feel you care about
them Etck. Keeping it going a *little* longer than you
normally wld gives people the feeling that you are
Interested, Intrigued Etck, but there is a fine line
between that and keeping it going so long that you
start to look Mad, Obsessive, in Drug-Crazed Trance
Etck. If you are naturally Shy, you can make an Impact
with the opposite, viz: Lady Diana Spendthrift, who
Charmed the World by staring at her feet under
fluttering lashes Etck.

2) *Humour*. Don't just tell jokes. A V. Good one
occasionally, but if you do it all the time, the LURVE
object just feels they're in the audience at a show they
never wanted to go to. Humour shld emerge from
situations you are in, things you're talking about Etck,
and if you are good at that it is one of the best bits of
Personality, because it makes you seem Cool,
Independent, and Fun To Be With (NB you can also
seem Cool by the opposite method; maintaining

Spot the Personality Types that are working....

sombre, brooding, tortured Etck Personality that
speaks of visits to the Dark Shores of Life Etck. This is
useful ploy if you are striking-looking, but is not so
easy to keep up if you look like a gerbil Etck).

3) *Interests*. However sympathetic a listener you
want to show you are, no-one wants to feel they are in
the company of Little Noddy, so it is V. Imp to project
Interests of yr own to register yr Personality. It is
generally better for these to be such things as The
Environment, Reading, Mountaineering, Space Travel,
the Internet Etck than collecting bus numbers, football
stickers, first-edition Batman comics Etck, but of
course it takes all types.

Personality also includes items such as Charm, Good
Manners, Affability, Generosity Etck. These are not
always V. Good guides to character, as many an axe
murderer has lurked beneath a charming exterior, but
quite often it is the best guide you've got. And
therefore it is worth polishing the exterior so that V.
Handsome People (I mean V. Honourable people) will
be interested enough to search out the rough diamond
that nestles within.

*Forget the rest,
She's still
the best...* →

PETS

To LURVE an animal is V.V. Like LURVing a person
and V. Much easier in respect of clitorises, condoms,
STDs Etck, because if you have this kind of a
relationship with yr Cat, you should see somebody

about it and so should the Cat. A pet will do all the things you hope BOYZ will do but don't, ie: always be there when you call, sit on your lap for hours at a time (don't try this with yr goldfish), never disagree with a word you say, warm your bed if Hot Water Bottle bursts, Etck Etck. I never got the horse or the dog of my dreams (the one that wld rescue me from snowdrifts, introduce me to boyz by tangling his lead in their dogs' lead like in *101 Dalmatians* Etck) which is prob why I called my long suffering but beLURVEd cat Rover.

They say that losing pets is a V. Good preparation for life's Hard Blows, also. But although the funeral of Benjy's goldfish was one of the saddest moments of my life, I'm not convinced that waving a tearful farewell to a matchbox (lined with rose petals, painted with *Cyril R.I.P.* and launched on Thames in driving rain) is, however affecting, a genuine preparation for the mortality of Major LURVEd ones like Granny Chubb. Also, if Benjy's reaction is anything to go by, the Young are V. Sooperficial. He cried for two hours, had a strawberry ice cream and never mentioned Cyril again.

PETTING

This does not mean cuddling up to Yr Hamster in the back row at the Odeon, but is an old-fashioned and V. Nice way of saying canoodling, kissing, fondling, snogging Etck. Phew . . .

POETRY

Poetry is changing in the late 20th C. LURVErs are less likely to moon around the woodlands wearing figleaves Etck and going on about Dante and Beatrice as they are to recite something like the following:

(Spoken fast in ragga accent over loud repeated bassline and drums)

Tigress! Tigress! burning bright
Got to have you in the daytime, got to have you all de night
Goin' to shout it in de street, goin' to tell it to de nation
You got the LURVin' attitude to cause a conflagration
I don' min' you gettin' hot to shoot me balls off with a gun
I ain' goin' to tell the Five-O that you blew away your mum
In this cold world we got to make the heat we can
Tigress wrap your body round me LURVE
Let us boil up de story in de way that we began

Or something like that. Well anyway, times are changing. I can't imagine DH serenading *moi* like this, but I can't imagine him writing that he wander'd lonely as a cloud either.

Nonetheless, persevere. Many a heart has been stirred by a well chosen word. Viz Great poets, artists, playwrights Etck. If anyone laughs at your poetry it just means they have No Soul and you don't want to LURVE someone without a soul, do you?

PORNOGRAPHY

This has nothing to do with LURVE, but some people think it has to do with SEX, so I am including it briefly.

Even Benjy is beginning to notice that pix of Gurlz wearing what looks like V. Uncomfortable underwear and nothing else are now displayed all over Family Newspapers Etck, so mild Porn is pretty hard even for the V. Young to avoid.

But even if you think Page Three Porn isn't V. Serious, you have to accept that some Porn is V. Serious indeed, espesh for the people who appear in it. I read a V. Upsetting article about this recently which explained how women and even very young children are forced to make horrible videos Etck, and some of this stuff was unspeakable and truly cruel. I hope none of you dear readers will ever see things like this or have ever been involved. If you have, you need help. See confidential phoneline number at end of book.

PREGNANCY

You are in LURVE. Or perhaps you are in LUST. Things develop fast and before you know it you are Doing it with a Boy who doesn't carry Condoms! How can this be?! Can this be happening to Sane, reliable, responsible YOU?

Sadly the answer is yes, as at the height of passion, it is sometimes V. hard to stop. Heed L. Chubb's advice: This can happen to anyone but it is YOU who will be holding the baba. Be Prepared. Carry a Pack of Three, or a Pack of Ten if you think you're not going to be interrupted for that long. Don't dally with a boy who doesn't. Don't be pressured.

The Teenage Worrier who thought the Rhythm Method meant doing it to music

There is Emergency Contraception that can be taken up to 72 hours after unprotected sex; ask your doc, fast. Wear sack over head or go to next town if you are too embarrassed to pick up leaflets about this stuff at the village chemist who has known your mum since she was mewling, puking Etck baba herself. If you do get pregnant, you will need advice as your decision will be V. hard. See numbers at end of book and also TERMINATION.

PROPOSALS

Range from 'Will you show me your bottom?' (Benjy to Older Woman – aged 7 – next door) to 'Will you fill the Abyss within my Soul and be my Life Partner?' (Daniel to *moi*, wish, sob, Etck.)

Main rule for successful Proposal, whether decent or indecent, is to have done yr best to discover beforehand whether the recipient is likely to have the slightest glimmer of interest in saying 'Yes'. So far, I have only discovered one question that is always answered in the affirmative, and that is when you are in someone's house and you ask them if you can use the loo. But I'm practising.

238

PROSTITUTION

This is a V. hard subject to wag yr finger about because it is the Oldest Profession and goes on because some men and Boyz have Worries about Doing It or can't find anybody to say Yes (or even less Yes Yes Yes), and as Ashley's economics books say, wherever there is a market, someone will provide the service.

Prostitutes sell sex. They are usually Gurlz, though more Boyz are doing it now and the clients are almost

always men. I think it is V.V. Unfair that there are no
V. sumptuous fountain-filled pleasure domes for us
Gurlz to go to, full of V. Handsome Young Men ready
to do our bidding Etck. I also think there is often not
much LURVE in the lives of prostitutes, and helping
to make their lives nicer by putting the business in the
High Street alongside Sainsbury's, Woolworth's Etck
might help. As things are, prostitutes start out full of
hope they can make loadsa dosh and get out quick.
They almost invariably end up wasted by drugs and
abusive pimps.

PUBERTY

This is when all the stuff that this book is about
actually starts to happen. Gurlz get periods and grow
Bazoomz (except in case of *moi*, moan, gnash, cruel
world). Boyz find their Willies get more unruly, their
voices break Etck. Hormones zoom about at a fearful
rate and cause V. Bad Moods and V. Strong Urges.

CHAPTER TEN QQQQQQQQZE TO SSSSSSSSSSSSSSSES

I have spent three days being sweetness and light to my Only Father. Cooked, washed, scrubbed, fawned Etck Etck. V. Exhausting. No luck. 15 is far too young to gad about airports grovelling after Evil Sex Machines from Hell who only want me for my bod Etck Etck. Moral: with some parents, Honesty is not always the best policy.

I begged and pleaded and finally I reminded him of how he felt about the Acrobat that he ran off with when I was 9. He went suddenly quiet. He looked wistful. He hummed a few bars of That Daring Young Girl on the Flying Trapeze. *He became Maudlin, wiped nose on sleeve Etck, said Love was a wonderful thing and asked if I was On The Pill, thus confirming that parents Only Think About One Thing. I said I was fully conversant with modern contraception thank you, but that I was saving myself for somewhere better than the Arrivals Lounge at Gatwick. He mentioned that Daniel had always seemed a solvent, er, he meant respectable, boy and that as long as I promised to be home by 10 pm I could go.*

My cup overfloweth.

The only blot on my horizon is Rover, who hasn't eaten anything (not even sardines with marmalade which she usually only has on her birthday) for two days. And she is looking V. Pale.

Winning over Father

QQQQQQQ

QUARRELS

The expression 'LURVErs' tiff' is used to demean the agonizing disagreements that dog passionate unions (or unite passionate dogs ho ho) and cause frenzied torrents of emotion, the throwing of breakable objects, returning of rings, tragic declarations of Imminent end of universe and immolation of participants Etck Etck. Just because these start in tears and end in reconciliation, vows of everlasting LURVE Etck, does not mean they shld be relegated to the status of tiff.

Even so, it is V. Imp to recognize the difference between the turbulent quarrel and the kind of deadly recrimination that precedes a real Break Up. This is like the difference between a fiercely fought football match (the quarrel) and a war zone (the Break Up) in which each party sees themselves equally aggrieved and betrayed. See BREAKING UP (sob).

RRRRRRRRRRR

RACISM

Mixed race LURVERs still have an uphill battle

in some parts of Little Britain. I am going to rewrite Romeo and Juliet (an Irish Juliet and a Chinese Romeo? A Scottish Romeo and a Guyanese

Every prejudice... in ye humble opinion of El Chubb, is as foolish as the above...

Juliet? A Vietnamese Juliet and an English Romeo? –
maybe all six) to show grown-ups how V. Callous,
stupid, old-fashioned Etck their lousy prejudices are.

It is a tragedy that withered hands of bitter parents are still clutching at winged heels of young Lurve just because they want their son or daughter to marry someone who looks, speaks, acts like them. You'd think after their own parents had beaten the Nazis in a World War Etck, older generations wld know better, but no . . . Worse still, some YOOF are as bad!!!!! When morons wearing swastikas start wrecking football stadiums, it shows you have got to be on your guard . . .

RAPE

Not to do with LURVE or SEX, but Power. Rape is forcing someone else to have SEX when they don't want to. It's almost always done by men to women, it can be done by a complete stranger, or it can be done by someone you thought was a Friend, and who refused to believe you when you said NO. (The latter is now called 'Date Rape'.)

If you have been raped by a stranger or by someone you know, DON'T keep it a secret, however terrible it has made you feel because something awful has happened which you will need help and LURVE to get over, and the person who did it may do it again unless they're stopped. Don't keep it quiet because you know the person either, and are afraid of him, or he tries to convince you that he lost control beçause he LURVES you, or because you shouldn't have worn that blouse

Etck. None of these is the remotest excuse. For yr own sake, and for the sake of other Gurlz, and maybe even for the sake of the Boy in the long run, you shld always make a fuss and follow it up if this happens to you.

Hazel had a V. Frightening experience recently, where a man grabbed her from behind and pulled her into an alleyway with his hand over her mouth. She couldn't move and was incredibly lucky that another man just happened to come out of a gateway in the same alley. When he saw this, Hazel's assailant let go and said the following chilling words: 'She's my girlfriend – we're just having a row.' And then he WALKED OFF. He SAUNTERED off. Hazel was crying so hard that it took a while for the rescuing man to believe her story. By the time he did, they couldn't catch the attacker.

My mother says, that whenever you get a group of more than three women together, and start talking about such things, you will hear a story a bit like this one. I find this a V.V. Frightening thought. See phone numbers at end of book.

REINCARNATION

It is V. Fashionable to believe in reincarnation, and it can't be disproved. It also can't be disproved that there is a colony of purple elephants dancing the hokey-cokey in a giant jacuzzi under the surface of Mars, but no-one talks about *that*.

However, it is a V. Attractive Idea that you and your beLURVed have met in a Previous Life and will continue to meet for Eternity, being twin souls Etck.

REJECTION

You see the Object of your Heart's desire across a crowded room. You sashay up and use the chat-up lines you have been practising in front of the mirror for five years. Your desired One looks up absent-mindedly and his troubled brow breaks into radiant sunshine as he spies the Gurl of His dreams, standing two paces behind you.

This is Rejection. It is a thing V. Sad, but it is part of LURVE's hurly-burly. Your response shld be to gracefully hurl this burly oaf aside and move on to pastures new, other fish in sea Etck. If your LURVE is True (like mine, sob) you will have to join a nunnery and Do good Works. But it is V. Likely that you will recover. Meanwhile, for three months, don't go near open windows, railway tracks, deep water or lurving couples. See BREAKING UP.

RELIGION

One version of Religion is believing that Someone or Something bigger, smarter, more principled and Who has read a lot more books than Yrself and the rest of the

Yuman Race for that matter, is In Charge and you can safely leave the Big Decision to Him/Her/It. Whether Buddhist, Muslim, Hindu, Christian, Jewish, Rastafarian or whatever, Religion plays a V. Imp part in the lives of many people on the planet – both in poor countries, where maybe it gives Hope to people who otherwise haven't got anything, and in rich ones like America where some people seem to be V. Religious as a way of making sense of a World of Shopping that is Totally Naff and Incomprehensible otherwise.

Religion is about Dreamz and HOPE, and if The World'z Leaderz think those things are only about Shopping then we've all Had It. Don't be ashamed of feeling Religious; we are all Religious even if we don't believe in the One True God, because to be Yuman is to know you will one day Peg Out, but to imagine a world that nobody's invented yet but which may already exist in a place just around the corner. If you feel something deeply that yr Frendz mock you for, tell them to Get Stuffed, jump in the lake Etck.

BUT (NB This is V.V.V. Big But) L. Chubb sez, do not get involved in Lurve bombing Cults run by rich fat men covered in Rolexs who tell you they are God, or know a Man Who Is. These guys often talk of Lurve and the One True Way when all they want is slaves to do their bidding, give them all their dosh Etck. They can come V. Well disguised, either as poor or kind people, and often give Teenage Worriers the hope of a Family better than the one they have already (or perhaps have never had). DO NOT GET INVOLVED.

Beware Cults. Their leaders may resemble bank
managers. This does not mean they are responsible
Etck. Or they may look like kindly hippies. This also
does not mean they are responsible Etck.

If you have spiritual yearnings, choose a religion with a
long history in which you will not get brainwashed
against yr will. And steer clear of any that go in for
Hell fire or Damnation. What kind of an
all-LURVING God is that????? See GOD and JESUS.

REVENGE

I am a V. forgiving, kind person but here are some of
the fantasies of star-crossed vengeance I have dreamt of
wreaking:

1) Fill all Daniel's pockets with mixture of
frogspawn and gerbil poo.

2) Ditto Aggy's pockets.

3) Attach 'I must stop playing with my Willy' notice to the back of Daniel's coat.

4) Send note to Aggy as from DH saying he dreamz only of her Coming To Him in a black binbag with holes for the Vital Partz, and fifty invites to DH's parents' wedding anniversary for the same time and place.

5) Forge letter from DH's headteacher to his parents, regretting his abuse of small boyz on the playing fields and telling of yr sad intention to expel him.

ROMANCE

Romance puts a bit of magic and spice into yr Life, a spring in yr step, makes you walk around with daft ecstatic smile on face Etck. It doesn't have to be about LURVE, it can be about the countryside in spring, yr gerbils nesting, yr parents going two days without an argument Etck. But because Romance is about looking fondly and affectionately at Life, some people think there's something wrong with it – like it's sentimental about something or somebody so you can't see Things As They Really Are. But how do we know when Things are what they Really Are? (This is a V. Imp, deep question of philosophy, which I will come back to when I get a chance to write a book longer than the Bible Etck, and a better edukashon than Slugg's Comp for that matter.)

However, because all our favourite stories are about getting hold of LURVE and with it the keys to Happiness, we don't often pause to think whether it is possible to be Happy without LURVE (or at least one Special LURVE) in our lives.

I am V. Worried about this, because I am In LURVE and therefore can think of V. Little Else. But from time to time dear reader, I pause to think that maybe Romantik LURVE is not all it's cracked up to be, and that perhaps a nice Person who CARES but who doesn't fill yr entire Emotional Horizon, plus a good balance of the other Imp things in Life, like a Healthy Bod, Interesting Work, good Frendz Etck make a lot more sense in finding yr way through Life's murky tapestry.

Still, I dream of waterfalls, mountains Etck through which Daniel and I gallop on our wild white steeds to do daring nookie under the stars. Also of big bunches of flowers, chocs by the sackful Etck . . .

See also VALENTINES.

SSSSSSSSSSS

Scandal

I must say I Laughalot when Cabinet Ministers who go round saying everyone shld respect Marriage Vows, Family Values Etck turn out to be keeping Secret LURVErs in fur-lined left-luggage lockers in Victoria Etck, and maybe they deserve it for being such Hypocrites. But generally scandals about LURVE in Brit papers are about making something naughty/dirty/sniggery/mucky out of it, just like ancient 'Carry On' films about Berms, Bazooms, Pantsdown Etck. El Chubb motto: what people do in their bedrooms, and who with, is their Own Business! (Though if their Bimbos, Himbos, maids, butlers, gerbils Etck tell the Press, I shall of course be forced to read it as research for Campaign.) Even if they are World Leaders, have their Finger on the Button Etck, there is no evidence that it makes them any worse at a job they're probably pretty bad at already.

**Winter V.Good if you are more confident re: your
personality than yr looks...**

SEASONS

Ye changing seasons have a V. Big effect on Pashione.
Spring and Summer are favoured months for inspiring
LURVE thoughts, because even in grey old Britland
people wear less then, and yr Juices Etck start pumping
into Vital Partz, putting a telltale glitter in the eye and
so on. You can, of course, lie around under hedges in
parks Etck during the summer, and if you can avoid
rolling into something yukky, it can be a V. Nice way
of both communing with Nature and being with the
BeLURVed at the same time, though you have to be
careful not to get too Carried Away, or else you will
indeed be Carried Away by the Forces of Law Etck and
sentenced to six months under a cold shower.

SELF-DEFENCE

Self-defence (Judo, Karate, Jiu Jitsu, I Kiku, Flying Ef
Yu, Hee Nut U Etck) isn't usually necessary in LURVE
circs, unless you have changed yr mind about someone
and he won't take no for an answer, in which case a deft
smack in a vital Bit might be a last resort. But it is a V.
Good idea for Gurlz to learn judo or karate in case of
assault which can happen to anyone. Campaign for
Alarms, Etck for all gurlz to carry!

SEX

I hope you didn't turn to this section first, because sex has to be seen in the full and rich context of a lustful, I mean LURVing, relationship. Once you are over 16 it is no longer illegal to Do It, (unless you are a Gay Boy, moan, whinge, unfair Etck) though as El Chubb has

stated elsewhere in this Vital Tome, nobody shld feel pressurized to until they're ready because it isn't obligatory and only Geeks and Nerds think the worst of you if you don't.

I always know when my Beloved Parents are contemplating this V. Rare event because my father starts screwing (sorry) the broken lock back on to their bedroom door about midnight and then cuts himself, thus causing more disturbance than the soundtrack of an Adult Movie played at 5 mill decibels. Then he gives up and tries to drag the chest of drawers in front of the door, putting his back out and waking the entire street with bellows, curses Etck. By this time my Dear Hopeful Mother is fast asleep. I think he may think of the Acrobat at these times.

If you DO feel ready for SEX, these are some things to explore, SWOOOON, chance wld be FINE THING Etck.

Foreplay. If your beLURVed thinks this means watching Match of the Day before Doing It, you might want to look at yr Relationship again. Foreplay means discovering all about each other's erogenous Zones. Most Teenage Worriers have these all over, so they aren't hard to find. Many Boyz go straight for nipples Etck under the impression that twiddling them will Turn You On like a video, and Boyz sometimes complain (so I understand) that Gurlz yank their Willies like gear-levers, so a little sensitivity is needed all round. A few hours spent fondling a wrist, frinstance, can be V. Exciting if the wrist is attached to the Right Person. And it is worth remembering that Foreplay, Kissing, Exploring Each Other (phew, mop brow Etck) is still SEX all right, so you are still entering into this V. Exciting Grown-up world even if you are not technically Doing It, and it is a lot safer to experiment with until you settle down with a more regular partner, have some idea about their previous SEXlife, understand yr Emotions better Etck.

259

Safe SEX is now a phrase you hear a lot. SEX has never been safe, since Gurlz cld always get pregnant with babies they didn't want, and both parties cld catch infections, not to mention the Emotional Risks in V. Intense SEXual relationships anyway. But now there is AIDS (see STDs) which has already killed a lot of people, and which is mostly contracted through SEX.

Many Teenage Worriers are also convinced that they will be unable to have children, either because they haven't had their periods, or they have teensy bazooms, titchy hips, huge bazooms, hairy chests, teeny willies, knock knees, must be hermaphrodites, or (daftest of all) it runs in the family. Do not fall prey to this misconception, as twere. Teenage Years are the most fertile of yr Life for reproduction of Ye Species, and one

lucky escape does not mean you can't conceive a little replica of yourself (or worse, of Syd Leer with whom you went a Little Bit Too Far behind Jackie's mum's sofa). CAMPAIGN FOR SEX TUTORS ON NATIONAL CURRICULUM NOW. Etck.

SHOES

V. Comfy. But is it Romantic? (worry, worry)

There is only one pair of shoes that a Teenage LURVEr can poss be seen in and that is the Brand New Lite Jackal Tri-Stars which play rap tracks according to yr walking speed and light up like Christmas trees. I have been saving for a pair of these to replace my DMs for two weeks, ever since they first hit the shops and even my Guilt about Granny Chubb's glasses cannot divert me from this misson. I *have* to have those shoes. I *cannot* be Kool without them. I cannot be happy for a moment till I have them. I would die for them. I would kill for them.

Yes, dear reader, this is L. Chubb speaking . . . or it could be. Kids have been killed for their shoes before now. Get designer labels into perspective. You can't fall in LURVE with shoes, although it's true I did used to say a tearful goodbye to each year's pair of sandals from the age of 6 to 10, plus, shoes go everywhere with you, don't talk back (yet), kick yr enemies, support you through thin and thick . . .

People do not fall in Lurve with their shoes... I think

Arrrg. I'm weakening. Join L. Chubb's anti-fashion
campaign now before shoes turn into people and take
over the world. See FASHION.

SKIN

Anyone who has read a single article in health magz will know that to keep their skin silky smooth as a telephone receiver they need to eat well, sleep well, exercise regularly and clean their mug. That's it (except for minor fact that most of us have suppurating morasses of sandpaper and pustules where our faces shld be).

> Q: What does a Teenage worrier's Skin have in common with the Middle East?
>
> A: Deserts, oil wells

Why then, do *Smirk*, *Weenybop* Etck bombard us with oceans of potions and lotions? Because, dear reader, they do not care about US but only about their advertisers – and if they do not try to convince us that just one more dollop of *Luminata* will make us glow like dew at dawn in Spring Meadows, then the nasty firms who make the wonder creams Etck will pull out their advertisements and the ickle magz wld go down the plug. Good thing too, save trees (but what about all those poor workers who slave to make the creams and write the magz? Guilt, writhe Etck).

SLIMMING: see DIET

SMELLS

The smell of the human Bod is V. Imp in Sexual
Arousal but you'd never think it if you just read the
deodorant or perfume ads, because they all make it
seem as if people won't come within a bus-length of
you unless you have zapped every crease and fold of yr
Bod that might conceivably smell of anything but pine
trees. Teenage Worriers the World over are responsible
for zillions of quid going down drain on sweat-and-
pong zappers of all kinds. Naturally, the eco-conscious
nineties Worrier will know that if you must use one of
these, you use a roll-on rather than an Ozone-
destroying spray. But certain scents are V. Imp in
attracting LURVErs, and too much squirt-on scent can
make you smell like something normally used to clean
the lavvy, so don't overdo it. Don't be tempted to buy
deodorants for your Naughty Bits, either. It can upset
the natural balance of The Fluids (cor, phew, slurp,
cross legs Etck) and cause soreness and V. Strange
Mutant Smells that might possibly trigger
Embarrassing Chain Reaction, such as your mother
calling in the pest control Dept Etck.

Most commercial pong reducers won't give you any
more benefit than a good sluicing in Our Gorgeous
Privatized Water. One of my nightmares is that the
Middle Classes will start using Mineral Water for

washing soon and then the rest of us will have our supplies metred and only have enough for half a cup of tea and a boiled egg every second Thursday. See also NOSE, PERFUME.

SPERM

This is the zillions of little seeds that come shooting out of a Boy'z willy when he Ejaculates, has Orgasm Etck Etck, which of course only happens when he is deeply in LURVE, profoundly spiritually moved Etck, and never has anything to do with the picture of Sharon Grone in a scene from her latest movie *Basic Income* on Page Three.

A boy in the Fifth Year has attempted to count his own sperm under the microscope in the Bio Lab and is V. Depressed because he has so far failed to find any. The Boyz say this is because he's run out from firing it all over his bedroom, round the back of the bike sheds looking at *Rogue, Yob* Etck but he says it's because the cheapskate school buys its equipment in the Action Aid shop to save money and the microscopes aren't powerful enough to catch all the zillions of leaping, wriggling thingies milling about in his Humanity-Saving sample. When Boyz think about Doing It, what the Sperm is actually for is the last thing they're interested in, but they do worry about how much of it actually comes out, as if this is a sign of how much of a Hunk they are. Usually a Boy Doing It (with himself

Sperm School

or somebody else) will produce approx 3 millilitres of seminal fluid, which is the white stuff the sperm swans around in. This contains about 100,000,000 spermlets! (Arg, contraception, nunnery Etck.)

STDS (SEXUALLY TRANSMITTED DISEASES)

There are V. Good leaflets in your doc's surgery about these and I have smuggled several dozen out and discovered chlamydia (which I thought was a houseplant), trichomonaisis, herpes and many other varieties that will keep a Teenage Worrier awake at nights.

You can't get Sexually Transmitted Diseases from thinking Rude Thoughts, but you can get them from Sex, so naturally the simple way to avoid these infections is Not to Do It. This is a course I have been forced (I mean, I have Nobly Chosen) to take. But it is not a strategy that can be relied on to last for young LURVers, so it is V. Imp to BE SAFE.

The most Worrying STD is the HIV virus which causes AIDS, and despite the increase in the heterosexual population of this incurable disease, V. Few Teenage Worriers seem to think it could happen to them. I find this V. Odd, since Worrying about whether our hair is too greasy, or whether we shld wear a nose stud Etck consumes vast tracts of our time. It is V. Imp to remember that you can't get the HIV virus from loo seats, hugging Etck as the virus which causes AIDS is V. fragile outside the human body. You can get it from Sex, though, and it is another essential reason to use condoms as well as to stop a baby. See Phone numbers at end of buke.

SUICIDE

As far as I know there is no record of anyone dying of a broken heart. There have been cases of Teenage Worriers killing themselves before their hearts have had time to mend, though. Overdoses are the most common method used by Teenagers and these are often decried by the adult world as 'cries for help'. After which – apart from stomach pumps and general survival techniques – not enough help of the right kind is often given. If anyone is unhappy enough even to take a small overdose, it means they are in a V. Bad way and need tons of support. It is also V. Imp to tell someone if you have taken an overdose, even if you didn't lose consciousness, felt OK and changed your mind about dying. Because it is quite possible to seem OK for a few days and then die of liver failure after taking too many painkillers or something.

Sometimes there can be a chemical imbalance that could be set right and this does not mean that you are inadequate, just that your body is a bit short of something it needs. You wouldn't feel guilty if you needed water after two days in a desert, so it's daft to feel guilty about needing other things to make you feel better, as long as they are legal and prescribed by a doctor.

Do not be afraid of any kind of therapy, counselling, or support. You may need several kinds of help at once if you are feeling this bad. And if you get them you will look back on this horrible time as if it were a bad dream. See phone numbers at end of book.

CHAPTER ELEVEN
TTTTTTTTTTEEEEEEZE to WWWWWWWZ

God can't be failed Stand-Up Comic because I have heard that even V. Sick comedians reckon it's bad for their careers to make jokes about animals dying. I am now like Indiana Jones when hanging on by his fingertips to tailboard of speeding truck driven by cackling Nazis and being pursued by shoal of piranha fish on motorbikes who will eat him in a flash if he falls off. It is one of those situations where whatever decision you take it's AGONY. Where there seems to be no way out but down Etck.

I was so V.V. Worried about Rover that I brought her to the Vet, who said he thought we were going to Lose Her. Her only chance is an Emergency Operation for which my father says he'll take out a second mortgage if necessary.

Rover has the operation today at 4 pm. Daniel's plane arrives at 1600 hrs. According to my calculations (I spent ages looking at the 24 hr clock trying to work it out) 1600 hrs and 4 pm are exactly one and the same time.

My father says he will sit with Rover and hold her paw. When she heard this, she threw me a yearning look, I swear it. As if to say, you go, leave me here, I'll be OK, get on with your Life Etck, I'll only Slow You Down . . . sob, weep, sniff Etck.

But, Oh, Reader(s), of course I couldn't do it. I HAD to leave my father and Benjy in front of Kids TV and take Rover to the Vet myself. We went via Spiggy's, and I decided to subject her to the Supreme Test of Teenage Worriers'

Friendship. She was surprised to be asked to take a cab to Gatwick at such short notice to meet Daniel instead of me, specially as I haven't seen her since That Fateful Day, but she has true Flying Doctor's blood. I thrust her my mother's secret stash of cash she keeps for emergencies in a small purse under the bin-liner in the kitchen bin (it is V. Good way of ensuring nobody nicks it unless it is A Real Emergency) and gave her the Vet's address, so Daniel could come straight there if things had gone horribly wrong and Rover was at Banana's door. But at least someone I trusted wld meet DH off the plane and he wld know I Lurved him still.

Weeping, paw in hand, Rover and I entered Dr Sprout's surgery. I sat with Rover while he put her under anaesthetic and fainted at once. I woke up to find Rover and Dr Sprout bending over me looking V. Worried; Rover, if anything, looking revived by the anaesthetic. Dr Sprout said she was fitter than she looked and gave her a bit extra, then he put me in the corridor to wait . . . 'Don't Worry,' said Dr Sprout as I wept copiously on to his jacket, which smelled of very old dogs, 'I'll call you in if it looks like we're going to lose her.' Lose her? Rover? Don't WORRY? How could I have entrusted Rover to this monster?

My happy years with Rover flash before me. The day I first saw her, in a nest of tissue paper, on my 7th birthday . . . her as a kitten unravelling balls of wool with Granny Chubb chasing her with a carpet beater . . . her pouncing on clockwork mice . . . the soft sound of her wheeze on my pillow . . . her indifference to the blandishments of humanity (except mine) . . . want my Mum . . . the seconds tick past like centuries . . .

My life with Rover flashes before me...

Dr Sprout's face is a mask of tragedy when he emerges and I am crying too much to hear him at first. Then he takes an indigestion tablet and looks happier. All I hear is him saying 'Poor old Mog'. I hate the word 'mog'. Then I realize it's just his cheery Vetspeak banter. Rover was bouncy as a new born, right-as-rain Etck Etck. Dr Sprout suggested I sue the catfood manufacturers for allowing bits of Lego into their tins. So that was it! He'd never come across it before . . . but once the obstruction was removed, Rover was like a new cat. My Cat is Reborn, Daniel is on the way home to my arms, my cup runneth over Etck.

But who was the Lego culprit? Benjy! As I trudged home, cherishing my cat basket with its happy burden, I wondered if you could sue your little brother for negligence. I think I'll send him an official letter from Chubb, Chubb, Throttle and Chubb written on my Adored Father's computer and see if I can frighten him.

Once I'd settled Rover, I dashed off to telephone the airport. Daniel's plane was delayed TWELVE hours. My father, recovered from his brief bout of bonding with his only-daughter-in-the-world, put his hoof down firmly at any suggestion of me going to hang around by the runway all night. So I left a yearning message on Daniel's parents' ansaphone, asking him to come round whatever time of day-or-night it was Etck. My money ran out before I had Declared My Lurve in all its full glorious poetry Etck. For a TEENAGER-IN-LURVE, to be without a telephone is like a musician without an instrument, a painter without a brush, a gerbil without a loo roll.

Tried to sleep . . . wrote this instead.

TTTTTT

Teeth

Keep them clean. All other cosmetic hope may as well be abandoned as yr av dentist will refuse you any treatment on the NHS the second you are 16. Even *on* the NHS dentists are V. Expensive which is why the Americans (who all have private health insurance which costs them a Fortune) reel backwards at the sight of our mossy gums and murky molars as though we lived in Dark Ages. I wore a V. disgusting brace from the age of 8 until last year. The dentist said I shld wear it for even longer, but it is asking too much of yr averagely vain LURVEr to clash braces. Kissing properly is hard enough work as it is, and clashing EMbraces is more my style (writhe, flush).

TELEPHONE

A Teenager-in-LURVE with no Telephone is a Tragik Thing indeed. A Teenager-in-LURVE *with* a telephone is worse. No-Telephone LURVErs whine, rage and rail against the Fates preventing them from speaking to their beLURVEds 24 hrs a day. LURVErs With telephones rail and sob and Wait for LURVErs that don't ring. The most Tragik case of all is the case of *moi*

Benjy's had a Mobile Phone since he was two...
why not moi?

— whose telephone is cut off two or three times a year
for several weeks because her adored Father has pushed
the bill down the back of his desk and has run out of
money by the time the Final Demand hits the doormat.
This means I wait by the phone for several days before I
realize the reason it isn't ringing is because it can't.

Mobile phones are now getting so cheap that Benjy
will soon be able to have one by just putting his X on a
rental agreement and pledging Horace as security. El
Chubb will have one and then there will be No Escape
from my LURVing enquiries, and no excuse not to call
back. There will also be no moonlit walks without
Adored Mother ringing to check I am wearing a
jumper, but perhaps soon it will be possible to hire an
answering service staffed by out-of-work actors who
imitate yr voice saying yes, I am wearing three layers of
woolly body-condoms to guard against all likely
accidents, and I'll be back by 10.30 for my hot choccy.

TENNIS

Shld you be a Sporty Type, the tennis lawn is a fine
venue for showing off thighs, knickers Etck and many a
True LURVE has ignited over the volley of a frolicking
ball, esp when the Umpire declares 'LURVE all'. Slurp.

TERMINATION

This is the more cosmetically acceptable term for
abortion, a horrible word suggesting knitting needles,
Victorian backstreets Etck. Either way, it means ending
a pregnancy and is one of the things my mother has
always been V. Outspoken about. She went on all those
Women's Right To Choose marches thousands of years
ago in the '70s, which were about making Abortions
safe and early and about decisions being made BY
women rather than by old blokes in white coats who
said things like 'who's been a naughty girl then?' and
not having the slightest idea what recommending a life
of nappies, sleepless nights, misery Etck meant to a
Female Person left Holding The Baby on her own in a
crummy flat the size of a matchbox and almost too
Young to do her own shoes up.

But although I rail against the Moral Majority and
think my Mum is absolutely right, I still wonder if I
wouldn't go through with it and have the baby adopted
and afford happiness to some childless couple Etck
Etck.

Considering either of these options makes me feel V. Queasy which is the best reason for having the safest possible sex or, like *moi*, moan cringe, not having sex at all. See other entries, if you'll excuse the phrase, for alternative kinds of safe sex, like taking your clothes off to look at *Baywatch* with the central heating turned up, or total antidotes to sex of any kind, like watching *Blind Date*.

What I was surprised to find out, is how many women *have* had abortions. Many of the mums you know probably have, but don't ask them, it's not perlite. There are, however, a lot of sensible and experienced people around who won't wag their fingers at you, and if you are in this situation you need help V. Fast. See advice numbers at end of book.

TESTICLES

← No, no! This is a TENNIS ball from page 277

More usually known as 'Ballz', these are the two hard lumps of tissue (animal tissue, not Kleenex tissue, stoopid) enclosed in a bag called the scrotum which hangs behind the Willy in Boyz. Ballz is usually used as a swearword, like so many things to do with Doing It. The Ballz are the clever devices that make the Boyz' Sperm. The bag apparently tightens round the Ballz when Boyz are in Sexually Arousing Circs (viz. seeing El Chubb wearing nothing but a see-thru binbag, white ankle-socks and a cloche hat, oh really, more like Sharon Grone wearing only scarlet stilettos Etck). Ballz are really sensitive anatomical partz, and V. Painful if struck hard by anything, and while this might V. Occas be useful as a last line of self-defence in case of violent assault, it is not recomm. for just playful joshing with yr BeLURVEd or you cld find yr chances of a fruitful SEXual partnership becoming V. Bleek.

THEATRE

Interlekshual LURVErs may like to swap the demands of French Cinema for an evening at one of our many great theatres. It's not so easy to wriggle the hands into V. Int places unobserved like in the back row of the Blogsworth Essoldo, but being a posher occasion can make you feel V. Classy and Glamm, which can be almost as much fun. *Haardon Aarsz* ice-cream may be served in the interval, programmes double as exquisite souvenirs of a wonderful evening, and the play might be interesting, too.

At Hazel's posh Gurlz' Academy they are always swanning off to the theatre but Sluggs Comp know that 98% of the parents can't afford the tickets, even at reduced rates, so all we get is the odd visit from a mangy juggler or a Theatre in Edukashon team who explain all the scenes to you as if you were a Fule.

NB First Nite Outfit tips so people think you're a star:

1) Skimpy black gownless evening strap.

First nite outfit (+ wig)

Normal day-wear

Take-me-out-to-dinner Shoes

The transformation of Maureen Scroggs

2) Berm-length blonde wig.

3) Shimmery item at neck (sadly, *The Walrus and the Carpenter* forbids *moi* from wearing pearls).

4) Keep flashing piranha-like smile.

Do not shield face from photographers; stars like to be snapped at first nights and hover irritably unless cascades of flash bulbs explode as they appear. New photographers will think you are a V. famous person they shld know about, and will take yr picture so as not to be Left Out. This may get you on front of paper as 'Mystery beauty' and will certainly impress yr beLURVEd, especially if he has only seen you before with your normal spaghetti-like wig and wearing the L. Chubb outfit described in FASHION, above.

TRAPEZE ARTISTS

V. Dangerous, threatening species, Poetry in Motion Etck. My father ran off with one, spangly leotard and all, when I was 9. I think he tried to convince my dear mama that it was a Higher Thing (element of truth, given her profession) but I've seen the faraway look that comes into Boyz' eyes at circuses, and I think he liked the way the spangly leotard disappeared into her Berm. It is not V. Uplifting to have these thoughts about one's Dear Father, but maybe it is as well to be Realistic.

Anyway, his departure was brief. She left *him* for a snake charmer (Boyz, please keep jokes on this subject to yourselves) and it has scarred our family for life. Good Heavings! An insight! Maybe that explains Benjy's fear of floors; perhaps he dreams the only place he can be Truly Happy is trapezing eternally above distant cheering throngs, walking on the ground is like being a mermaid on land to him.

TYPES

If you are a would-be-Teenager-in-LURVE with a lot of LURVE to give but no-one to give it to, you shld learn to recognize various types. These are Unisex guides:

1) GOD'S GIFT (GG)

Usually V. Good looking with ear-to-ear smile, roll-on tan, sunflecked limbs etck. GG will be found in the middle of a large group of admirers, but as many of them will have fainted, you might be able to squeeze through to get a look.

2) INTERLEKSHUAL (IQ)

IQ is tall, skinny with knobbly protuberances (rather like *moi*, ahem) and a stutter. They will be V. nervy and Insecure about everything except their Brain Power and will not lift their Nose out of a book for long enough to survey the talent which means you have a good chance of beating any competition if you get in first.

3) YOB or LURG

Linguists will have noticed yob spells 'boy' backwards, so it is not surprising that it usually means Backward Boy. There are plenty of Gurlz in this category also, however, who enjoy chortling at everyone else's shortcomings except their own, so in the ints of Fair Play Etck I have introduced 'Lurg' which will soon catch on for the female of the species.

Yobs & Lurgs travel in gangs of a dozen or so, on account of needing this much combined Brainpower to keep their legs moving. They LURVE to insult opposite sex with cries of 'Dyke' or 'Poof', and think a good night out is throwing up over each other in the chippie.

4) DREAMER

This type is often V.V. Attractive, having vast orbs of eyes that gaze meltingly at you even while you are

Dreamer

picking your hooter. Wafting about vaguely makes them look like they are Playing Hard to get, but their charming smile, endearing habits Etck will soon pall when you have stood freezing for three hours at the appointed meeting place and they wander up and ask innocently, 'Is that really the time?'

5) *DYNAMO*

A whirlwind of efficiency and high achievement, the dynamo is that person who excels at team sports, wins swimming galas, plays piano to grade 7, helps old ladies, knows how to ski, is a black belt at judo, is a prefect, member of chess club Etck Etck and still gets a full hand of GCSEs. They will be more often loathed or admired than LURVEd however, so if your heart beats for a Dynamo, you're in with a better chance than you might think.

6) *STILL WATERS RUN DEEP*

This type is so V. Quiet that although they have been in the same class as you since primary school you have not noticed them – till now. Suddenly they have, well, blossomed. How come you never saw what fabulous eyes/figures/mugs/wigs Etck they had until now? Once caught, their loyalty is unswerving, I think.

7) *KOOL*

Kools never wear what everyone else is wearing; they are always on to the next thing. All shades of black suit them and they are often razor thin, and thus resemble

Kool (male)　　　　　**Kool (female)**

Human Forms cut out of old vinyl records. They care
enough about what other people think to want a
partner who is even Kooler than they are. So if you
really can't help LURVing a Kool, you will have to
spend 23 hrs a day getting the look right and the other
hour trying to get the Kool to notice you. Sleep
deprivation may help you achieve the strung out Look
(linguistic note: Kool, backwards), but if you have to
try that hard, you do not have what it takes to be a
Kool. This is known as a Paradox.

8) *NARCISSUS*

Greek Youth who was so captivated by his own
reflection in a pool that he fell in LURVE with himself.
If yr True LURVE is narcissistic, don't wear shades, he
will get too good a view of himself.

Narcissus

L. Chubb recommends that you give this type V.
Wide berth. (Is DH a Narcissist? worry worry, shades
of doubt Etck.)

9) *MODESTY INCARNATE*

MI is kind, thoughful, nice-looking, clean,
considerate and doesn't know the meaning of
boastfulness or pride. Sounds too good to be true? No
way. Two weeks of going out with MI will make you
long for Tarzan as they are so V. Insecure that you have
to spend nine minutes out of every ten bolstering up
their incy-wincy egos.

10) *MUSO*

Drummer, Sax-player, lead-Guitarist Etck. Don't
bother, as all the other gurlz/boyz/catz/gerbils Etck will
have got there first.

UUUUUUUU

Umbrellas

'U' looked a bit Lonely with just one entry, so I
thought I'd mention umbrellas also, as V. Good way of
getting to know LURVE object in rain-situations. Viz:
if you haven't met, you can introduce Self by laughing
charmingly as yr Umbrella blows inside out and nearly

pokes yr eye out. Finding cleft-chinned wunderbabes who have umbrellas however is prob thankless task, as they are more likely to be carried by Mr Bean types.

UNFAITHFULNESS

Fidelity has long been expected and required of women, while men are supposed to go off, sow wild oats, marry, father sons and heirs and then resow oats. The reasons usually given for this double standard go something like this:

1) Men have more powerful sexual drive, therefore need to Do It more.

2) When women have babies, their attention drifts off SEX (and their husbands) leaving poor male in need.

This looks V. Like a list that has been written by Men, to see just how much they can get away with. My experience of Gurlz is that they have V.V. Powerful Sex Drives too, though are more choosy. Some Boyz give the impression of wanting to Do It with anything that moves, or even doesn't.

My Adored Mother, in more confiding moments, has announced that women are usually so knackered after having babies that Doing It is usually the last thing on their minds. Also, I suppose their infants, with their soft curls, downy cheeks Etck, who LURVE them unreservedly, might be more attractive company than a farting heap of bristly excess flesh asleep among a pile

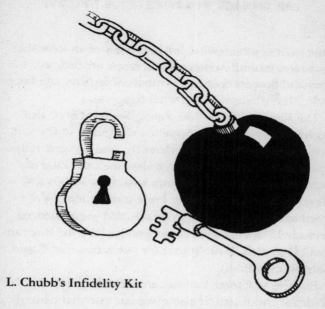

L. Chubb's Infidelity Kit

of lager cans in front of the telly. As for *moi*, I would be too frightened of AIDS or losing Daniel, to let him off leash for a millisecond. And if he wandered, I'd be off. Jealous? Who? *Moi?*

VVVVVV

Vagina

If you just think of your Female part as something Babies can come out of after uncovered Willies have gone in, it is a somewhat limiting view of an item that has been gracefully celebrated in erotic art Etck as byootiful flowers opening, symbols of fertility and hope Etck. Nevertheless, this is what happens.

The Vagina (which, like Penis, Testicles Etck also has its swearword version spelled with most of the letters of 'Aunt' but said differently, and not generally repeatable to yr Aunt either, unless she's the kind of Aunt Teenage Boyz sometimes wish they had) is a V. Clever part of a Gurl'z Bod. For a start, it looks V. Small and inconspicuous in repose, and inexperienced Teenage LURVErs sometimes wonder how the Boy can possibly get his Willy into it (or out again, fear, Freud, male phobias Etck).

But the V. Clever Vagina can not only stretch V. Wide for childbirth, it also gives out essential natural Essences, Unguents, Oils Etck (during Foreplay, but also in Dreamz, or glimpses of sensuous Boyz' forms in hip-hugging stone-washed denim, sigh) to make everything V. Slippery and SEXy and comfortable (thinks: thank heavings we are near the end of this Buke, El Chubb cannot stand the strain of all this much longer without cold shower, enrolment on Outward Bound course Etck).

NB Some Worriers may worry what their Vagina looks like. V. Nice, is the only sensible answer. This is one bit of your bod you can rely on to do the business whatever it looks like. Phew, relief, strike off one from Worry list Etck.

VALENTINES

Feb 14. Vital date in LURVer's calendar, when birds were supposed to choose their mates. I did notice the pigeons looking a bit friskier than usual this Valentine's Day, but I didn't see any of them actually Doing it. Great thing about Valentines is they are anonymous which means you can send loads without any rude joshing, giggling Etck. Also, you can make up V. Daft things Viz: *Bunnykins loves Snugglums True*

Etck. Anything wld look better on a Valentine card
than Scarlett (moan, whinge, cruel fate, but at least I
am not called Roland Butter ha ha yeech). I am hoping
to get Daniel to call me Diamond as befits my dazzling
personality Etck (ha ha, if only, glume, moan).
Diamonds are V. Valuable and rare, and, being the
hardest things on earth (apart from the Sexual Org of
Daniel Hope when confronted with the Naked Allure
of *moi*, some hopes, grue, moan Etck), they are V.
Useful as well as V. Beautiful (like the Sexual Org of
Etck Etck).

Odd to think there was a time when no-one felt
particularly Romantik about Human LURVE. Ancient
Greeks were more interested in Divine LURVE,
and women just bundled about being tenth-class
citizens and bringing up the next generation. This
all seemed to change when Troubadors Etck
devised 'courtly LURVE' when swains wld humiliate
themselves to do the bidding of a Fair Lady
(usually someone else's wife). And today we are
lumbered with fluffy loominous pink bears saying
HUGGUMS. Plato wld turn in his cave.

VIRGINITY

Teenage Worriers used to be bullied into Chastity by
Parents, teachers, the Church Etck. The same people
who bullied them did their best to keep them
Ignorant of the Facts of Life at the same time (see

IGNORANCE). However, Virginity should be a free choice (as it is in the case of *moi*, ahem) and not something forced on us by Loopy Moral Majorities trying to keep us Pure Etck as though we were crystal streams until polluted by Sex.

In the USA Virginity has become a craze, and like hamburgers they are trying to export it. The True Love Waits movement makes its members (ahem) sign a declaration which *promises* ('to those I date, my future mate and my future children') abstinence until marriage! Arg. No wonder they haven't got anyone over here to do it yet. Keep yer options open, say Brit Teens. Naturally, there are loads more virgins around than ever admit it, espesh Boyz, who feel they are obliged to pretend they have waved their willies at zillions of gurlz, otherwise their daft mates will laugh.

WWWWWWW

WEDDINGS

OK, you can't really have a whole book about LURVE without mentioning weddings, engagements Etck. I have to admit it is still the dream of a V. Big number of Teenage Worriers to get rings on fingers, walk up aisles in Big White Dresses Etck. This is V. surprising in the face of the example of the Royal Family, politicians Etck, although I make an exception for

myself and Daniel, who will naturally tie the knot in a
V. unkonventional way (in a dewy glenn, watched only
by robins, deer and the world's paparazzi).

Arranged Marriages are still qu common in many
cultures and as yet I don't know if anyone's done a
survey of which kind of marriages are happier . . .

Please discuss and send your essays on the subject to
Unfaithful MPs Committee, House of Common
Behaviour, London.

WET DREAMS

These happen when Boyz have sexual dreams and
orgasm while they're still asleep. Ashley told me this

happened to him once while he was lying under only a sheet on the school trip to Italy and he was V. Embarrassed to wake up and find all his so-called Frendz taking photographs. Boyz could talk about this to their Fathers or Mothers if they wld like to, but there is hardly any need as it is completely normal and has been going on since the Human Race began; in fact it is the prelude to the Human Race being able to go on at all.

WILLY

Some people think that it is a bit Coy to use terms like this instead of 'Penis' Etck, but as El Chubb has already writ (see PENIS), Penis is not a word I much like, and I never hear it used by Teenage Worriers, whether bossy folk think they shld or not.

The Willy is usually qu small and modest when going about its usual business (peeing, quietly reading the paper inside yr Underpantz Etck) and becomes larger and erect in SEXually arousing Circs. This

TEMPORARY
ERECTIONS
DEMOLISHED
Tel: 01- 28 -

happens because the tissues inside the Willy are full of blud-vessels that expand in SEXual excitement. The machinery that makes it go up is not a reflex like jerking yr leg when the doctor bangs yr knee, but depends also on how a Boy is *feeling* – about his LURVer, about himself, maybe even about his Adored Mother and Father. Imagine if Tower Bridge only went up if it liked the look of the ship that was hooting hopefully at it, or if it hadn't gone up and down too many times yesterday!

El Chubb's research on this has, of course, been largely second-hand (moan, gripe, when-oh-when Etck) but I have heard that one of the things that most perplex and scare Teenage Boyz is that while their Willies leap up and down at the slightest provocation, sometimes nothing happens at all when they are finally in a silk-lined boudoir with the BeLURVEd they have Wanted All Their Lives Etck. This is V. NORMAL and nothing to Worry about. It is caused by the build-up of stress and tension now the Big Moment has finally arrived. The best thing to do is relax, cuddle, kiss Etck, and forget about the sleeping Willy until it eventually realizes what's going on and leaps out of bed, and into bed, as twere. Almost all Boyz and Men, if forced to admit it, wld say that this has happened to them at least once, and prob several times in their SEXual lives, and is just a part of being made male.

After a Boy'z orgasm, the Willy quickly returns to its usual shape, and if you are using a Condom (as you shld be) it is V. Imp for the Boy to squeeze it gently around the base so none of the contents can leak out, and withdraw the Willy slowly from the Gurl so that it can't slide off.

Fishing? Or his WILLY?

Whatever, it's a fib

The other big, or little, Boyz' Willy-Worry is SIZE. A V. Old Myth says that V. Big Willies are more exciting for Gurlz, more likely to make them go Yes Yes Yes Etck. Teenage Boyz can therefore get up to ridiculous things with their Adored Father's retracting steel DIY tape measure Etck. But most Willies are more or less the same average size, even on otherwise V. Big or V. Little Boyz, and this has been quite enough to produce:

1) a V. Large number of people in The World, and

2) a V. Large number of LURVErs, Teenage or otherwise, with V. Big smiles on their faces.

CHAPTER TWELVE
XYZ

Daniel arrived, dishevelled and gorgeous, at teatime yesterday. He flung his arms out and I hurled myself as if fired from a cannon Etck. Eyes tight closed in Eckstasy, I did not see his outstretched palms which I obliviously struck as if running into Star Wars-type Force Field, and bounced off like pingpong ball cast into Outer Darkness Etck. He had indeed arrived twelve hours late, hoping to see moi. He had met instead an extraordinary, enchanting Australian who had declared her undying love for him as soon as their Eyebeams Crossed Etck.

Aaargh! Yeech! Puke! Murder! Suicide! Etck!

It was a whirlwind romance, he knew, but sometimes Life Was Like That, wasn't it? Her name? Sarah.

Sarah Spiggott.

Spiggy.

Rotten, stinking, conniving, yukky, loose-limbed, groovy, witty, confident Etck Spiggy.

BETRAYED.

Oh, treachery!

To add insult to injury, Daniel berated me for my 20 min message on his parents' ansaphone which he said was 'cringe-makingly embarrassing and inarticulate' and which his mother had been convinced was some floozie of his father's since I had neglected to mention Daniel's name or leave my own.

How can I describe my response? To go from Ecstacy to Agony in a millisecond? For the Sun to turn into a Black Hole? I must reinvent language, banish Laughter from every other chap of this book (not that there are any other chaps in this book, or in My Life, either, moan, whinge) as now I realize that all humanity is chaff, dross Etck. And that my life is a charade, As Flies to Wanton Boyz Are We to the Gods Etck. That Shakespeare knew what he was on about. It is a pit into which I plunge, a tunnel devoid of light. I shall wind up my alphabet along with my hope. If others can benefit from it, so Be It. The Nunnery beckons once more.

XXXXX

X-RAY

This used to be the only word for X in my ickle tots' alphabet book and I wouldn't mind borrowing this power from Superman's eyes in order to undress a few LURVlies of my acquaintance, espesh Syd Leer, to see if his Willy is the Eighth Wonder of the World he says it is. Also to see what DH gets up to without *moi* (bleekness, glume Etck. Deep despond. Unhappiness haunts me for Eternity).

XXXXXXXXXX

Is also for kissing which tragically is an activity in which I will never again engage. Woe, dust cloth.

Ashes. Have just written once more to Archbish re-being Nun. Perhaps my last letter went astray? Or was eaten by Horace?

YYYY

YOGA

Yoga is reputed to be V. Good for LURVE because it is V. Good For Everything. It is the ancient Indian art of standing on yr head for hours, tying yrself in impossible knots, and going '*Ommmmm*' in V. Solemn voice while being laughed at by the builders on the scaffolding across the road.

ZZZZZZZZZZ

ZODIAC

It is just as well this tragic *denouement* to my Planz came when I had nearly finished my alphabet of LURVE, otherwise I wld never have had the heart to continue. Here is my revised, sadly disillusioned, Zodiac of LURVE. As you know, I do not beleeve in Horoscopes . . . but sometimes, I wonder.

LURVE ZODIAC

EARTH signs: TAURUS (moi), **VIRGO** (Hazel), **CAPRICORN** (My Only Father). All supposed to be compatible with each other OR

WATER signs: CANCER (Granny Chubb), **SCORPIO** (Brian Bolt), ← arg **PISCES** (Grandma Gosling). ↖

FIRE signs: ARIES (Aggy)), **LEO** (Brother Ashley), **SAGITTARIUS** ← (Daniel, yearn) go for each other OR

AIR signs: GEMINI (Benjy), **LIBRA** (Spiggy, glume) **AQUARIUS** (my Mum)

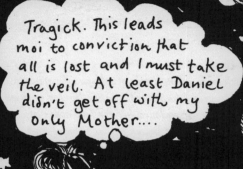

FINAL CHAPTER

I have been thinking.

Sarah Spiggott wrote a long letter of self-justification to Hazel, in which she said I had totally taken her for granted, exploited her friendship, abandoned her for five hours at Gatwick while I ponced about smarming at Daniel and betraying Aggy, wrecked her mother's trousers, and constantly made abusive and ignorant remarks about her Mother Country. And she hated being called Spiggy. She also loathed her own true LERVe being demeaned by my witty nickname of Malteser. She was also surprised at the remarkable lack of sympathy I showed when the Boy SHE lurved did not write. She had not even been able to tell me he had found Another, as I had been so obsessed with my OWN longings Etck Etck. For these reasons, she did not feel she had betrayed a True Frend. What is more, when she had been kindly helping me to entrap Daniel, she hadn't seen him. But the moment she laid eyes on him at Gatwick (when we went to see Aggy off), she fell more deeply in Lurve Etck Etck than she had ever known it was possible to feel. She never hoped for her Lurve to be requited until their eyes locked on his return. Since when she had been helpless with passion Etck Etck drone.

I made this letter into a paper dart.

Then I re-read it.

I must admit I squirmed at the barbed but undeniable

truth therein. I winced at the memory of all my Kangaroo-In-A-Basket jokes. I squirmed at my insensitivity re convicts, upside down surfers Etck Etck. Spiggy had been a pawn in my game. But she had made it to the back row and got to be Queen without any help from moi. *And, I had to admit it, Daniel Hope is so dazzlingly beeeeeyooootiful that everyone (nearly) does melt into a sticky goo on the floor at his gaze, cor, sob, sex, grrrr Etck. He can take his pick.*

I feel I shld tell Spiggy (I mean Sarah) that Aggy gave him the heave-ho (she's too brainy for him, really) and that his involvement is clearly a rebound. To love one who is so superficial has been my burden, but now the wool is drawn from my eyes etck and I can see the real DH. One who wishes only to be adored, and knows nothing of True Lurve.

It is great to be good pals with Aggy again and an additional reason for the lightening of my mood (ahem) is a sense that I have Matured. Daniel's Betrayal and Rover's brush with – banana – has scarred, but (ahem) Strengthened moi. *I feel that qu soon I will be able to say that word about dying that rhymes with breath and realize it is part of Life's rich pattern.*

There is also a V. Big Improvement at home. My Father's first (and only) Novel is about to be reissued and it means the phone is back on, my mother is back in the nest and we can afford to take Benjy on a tour of the flooring shops to choose something that he will be able to develop a Warm and Giving relationship with. My father is already assuming his book will become an Angry-Youth-Against-the-World type classic and get on the GCSE syllabus, but even I can see that it is more likely to be pie-in-the-sky than Catcher in the Rye. Still, it keeps us in Rice Krispies for a couple of months and Hope Springs Eternal Etck.

I had an Interesting Communication from Brian Bolt, too, in which he explained the incident with the flour and the bicycle tyre and suggested I accompany him to a seminar at the ICA. I've always preferred brains to brawn, but I think Brian may have been investing in an Exercise Programme. His arms are a shred less like fuse wire . . .

And Daniel?

I wld be with him now, perhaps, if I had not sacrificed meeting him because of my real True Lurve for Rover. And I am glad.

Because of all the mean, shifty things I have got up to in weaving my web to entrap him, only one thing makes me proud. I Stood By My Cat.

The End

(NEATLY)

HELP!

CONTRACEPTION, PREGNANCY, ETCK

Brook Advisory Centres
Contraceptive and counselling service for the under 25s. Local clinics throughout the UK. Under 16s can obtain confidential help.
020 7713 9000 (helpline, office hours)
020 7617 8000 (recorded information helpline)

Family Planning Association
020 7636 7866
(confidential helpline)

British Pregnancy Advisory Service
01564 793225

LIFE National Hotline
01926 311511
Will help if you have already decided to proceed with a pregnancy.

LESBIAN/GAY

Lesbian and Gay Switchboard
020 7837 7324 (24 hours, Mon to Fri)
Advice and info service that also offers advice for friends and family, nb: they are really hard to get through to, but don't give up.

North London Lesbian and Gay Project
020 7607 8346
Run the lesbian, gay and bisexual Youth Project for under-25s and can provide advice, info and education resources.

OTHER RELATIONSHIPS

'Who Cares?' Trust
020 7251 3117
Run by and for young people in care, aiming to make life better for them.

National Stepfamily
Association
020 7209 2460 (general
enquiries)
020 7209 2464
(confidential helpline)
*Advice for anyone on any issue
related to being part of a
stepfamily.*

HEALTH

HIV/AIDS

Confidential AIDS
Helpline
0800 567 123

Positive Youth
020 7835 1045
*Information and advice for
people under 25*

LOOKS

Eating Disorders
Association
01603 621414
Youth Helpline (18 years
and under): 01603 765050

Acne Support Group
020 8845 8776

ALCOHOL/DRUGS

Alateen
020 7403 0888
(confidential advice, 24
hours Mon-Fri)
*Specifically for teenagers
affected by the drinking
problem of a family member or
friend.*

Alcoholics Anonymous
01904 644026
If you have a problem.

Drinkline
Helpline: 0345 320202
(Mon to Fri, 9.30 a.m. to
11 p.m.; Sat and Sun, 6-11
p.m., all calls charged at
local rate)
Freephone 0500 801802
(recorded info)
*Very helpful with advice on
drinking levels Etck. Can send
you a free book, 'The Big Blue
Book of Booze'.*

ADFAM National
020 7638 3700 (10-5,
Mon to Fri)
*Run a national telephone
helpline for family and friends
of drug users so do contact
them if you're worried about a
mate or about a
brother/sister/parent.*

**Department of Health
National Drugs Helpline**
Freephone 0800 77 66 00
*A free and confidential service
open 24 hours a day, 365
days a year. Also available in
a range of languages other
than English. Free leaflets
and literature.*

Re-Solve
01785 817885
*Advice and information for
anyone involved in abuse of
solvents (inhalable things).*

VICTIMS

Childline
0800 1111 (freephone)
*If you or a friend have been
sexually abused, these people*

*will be very helpful and
sympathetic.*

**Campaign Against
Pornography**
Helpline: 020 7281 6376
*For anyone who feels they have
been injured/hurt/abused/
exploited through the use of or
making of pornography.*

**London Rape Crisis
Centre**
020 7916 5466 (office
hours)
020 7837 1600
(counselling)
*London-based but can refer
you to someone in your area
who can help.*

GENERAL HELP/
INFORMATION

The Samaritans
National Linkline: 0345
909090 (calls charged at
local rate from wherever
you call)

24-hour emergency service for the suicidal or despairing. A local number will also be in your telephone book or can be obtained by calling the operator. If in serious trouble, DO CALL.

Youth Access
0116 2558763
A service for all young people, referring them to independent local counselling services/advice centres Etck.

The information above was correct at the time of going to press. If any errors or omissions occur, Transworld Publishers Ltd will be pleased to rectify at the earliest opportunity.